# CREEPING CRAWLING CINEMA

By

Edward Brock

Published

by

## Mytholigious Press

## CREEPING CRAWLING CINEMA—A Prologue

Be they giant spiders, swarms of bees, blood-sucking ticks, slimy worms or intelligent ants, the "Killer Bug" movie has always been a particular favorite of mine. Beginning in the 1950's and continuing into the new century, the "Killer Bug" film has faded, only to rise again. Perhaps it's that inherent phobia of things with six legs, eight legs, 1000 legs, or no legs at all—and our attempt to face those fears—that keeps us coming back for more. Far better to watch them terrorize someone on the big screen than have to face them in our own bathrooms, bedrooms, backyards, city streets, or under our skin.

Whether it's Arachnophobia (fear of spiders), Myrmecophobia (fear of ants), Apiphobia (fear of bees), Vermiphobia (fear of parasitic worms), or the all-encompassing Entomophobia (fear of all insects)—most of us have experienced some form of that icky, skin-crawling feeling when a bug lands on you, or you walk into a spider web, or find a bite on you and not know how, or when, it got there. Though most of the time the fear is merely psychological, there are those moments when they are very justified—the Brown Recluse spider, the disease carrying tick, swarms of killer bees, skin-burrowing parasites—well, you get the idea. Now imagine swarms of these crawling on you in an attempt to eat, kill or change you. Or, imagine seeing them become the size of cars, becoming large enough to swallow you whole.

Enter the Hollywood filmmaker.

In the 1950's, Hollywood was working under the blanket of fear that every American was feeling–fear that the a-bomb would be our destruction. Is it any surprise that many films of the decade were subtle (and not so subtle) commentaries on those fears? It was inevitable that those fears would find themselves on drive-in screens and inside movie theaters— manifesting in the form of giant ants, spiders and other "bugs". The phobias already existed within us, so why not combine the two, Hollywood thought. Well, they did just that, giving us films that merged our atomic fears with the all too familiar and common bug phobias—and had us watch as those tiny creatures turned into killers. The Killer Bug genre continued to evolve. Those phobias and bugs found new ways to terrify us—nature gone wild, scientific experiments, insect intelligence, infectious diseases, and even bugs from other worlds made their way to the screen. It seems there was no place to hide once these tiny creatures took aim at us.

What I hope to do with this short little book, is familiarize you with this very fun and, sometimes, frightening niche. Starting in 1954 and diving into the B-level offerings on networks like the SyFy channel, I've chosen a selection of movies I believe are essential viewing for anyone interested in experiencing the sheer lunacy, silliness or goose-bumpy happenings in these films. As such, this is not a complete list of the killer bug films, but a sample of some of the best.

Some will make you cringe, some will make you laugh, and some will make you groan. But, it's still a fun little niche—that I hope never goes away.

# !!!!Spoilers Ahead!!!!

# THEM! (1954)

*"An Endless Terror! A Nameless Horror!"*

Director - Gordon Douglas

Writer(s) – Ted Sherdman / Russell S. Hughes (from a story by George Worthing Yates)

Starring – James Whitmore / James Arness / Joan Weldon / Edmund Gwenn

Distributor – Warner Bros.

Released - June 19, 1954

## Story:

After two New Mexico state troopers (Ben Peterson—portrayed by James Whitmore) and (Ed Blackburn—portrayed by Chris Drake) find a little girl wandering in the desert, they return her home—only to find the mobile home, where her family is staying, is torn apart. Her family is missing and only a single animal track is found.

Soon after, the troopers find a local a store owner dead, outside of his general store—which is also torn apart like the mobile home. Peterson leaves to check on the lost girl. Blackburn remains and soon hears a strange sound which seems to be growing closer. We hear his screams off-camera as he becomes another victim.

After sending a plaster cast of the strange footprint to Washington, D.C., an FBI Agent (Robert Graham—portrayed by James Arness) arrives to investigate—because they have no idea what the footprint is. He is accompanied by a doctor (Harold Medford—Edmund Gwenn) and his daughter (Pat Medford—Joan Weldon). After returning to the little girl's campsite, Pat Medford encounters a giant ant (over 8-feet tall). Her screams bring the others running and the police fire on it. Dr. Medford yells, "Get the antennae! Get the antennae!" and the police finally kill the giant creature after machine gun fire destroys the antennae. Dr. Medford is convinced that a colony of ants has mutated because of the radiation from the nearby atomic bomb tests before the Second World War.

Eventually, the ant colony is found and poison gas bombs on dropped on them. The ants are killed, but Dr. Bedford believes two queens have escaped. One is found in the cargo hold of a freighter and destroyed—the other has found its way to California.

The final act of the film finds the military and our intrepid heroes battling the giant insects in the drainage system of Los Angeles. During the battle, trooper Peterson is killed, and Graham is trapped in a cave in—but manages to hold off an attack by the giant ants, until he is rescued. The queen and her brood are finally destroyed using flame throwers.

The first film to merge the effects of the atom bomb, and one of our tiny little neighbors, *Them!* was a surprising success. During the film's early run, many film-goers were unprepared for what they were about to see—as promotional material kept the storyline vague (even releasing poster with nothing but text). They walked into the theater and after watching what seemed to be a crime thriller, were surprised—and thrilled, apparently—when the first giant ant makes an appearance. It worked, as movie fans flocked to it, making it one of the most successful films of the year for Warner Bros.

Like many monster movies, the actual creatures are not even seen until a quarter of the way in. The film was originally planned as a full-color, 3-D film, but numerous equipment malfunctions and budget cuts forced the filmmakers to use black and white (although the opening credit sequence still maintains the bright red title "THEM!").

As there was no CGI to rely on, the special effects crew (supervised by Ralph Ayers) built full-size props, and combined with some trick photography and miniatures, worked some magic that, although dated, holds up well as a representation of what quality effects could be in the 1950's. Though, as any special effects unit will tell you, the film was not without its screw-ups. The most blatant being a moment during the final battle where the mechanical innards of one of the ants can be seen (it was "fixed" in the DVD release).

The film was very popular amongst film-goers, which seemed to convince other Distributors to produce their own "big bug" movies. Today, the film is looked upon fondly by monster movies fans and sci-fi fans alike. And because it didn't play for laughs—as so many big bug films do these days—it is still one of the best representations of the atomic era monster movie. A solid beginning for the "killer bug" genre.

### *Cool Stuff:*

The film was nominated for an Oscar in Special Effects (it lost out to *20,000 Leagues Under the Sea-* 1954).

The loud, piercing sound the ants make upon approach is actually the amplified "singing" of tree-frogs.

The famous "Wilhelm Scream" was used during some of the action scenes.

The screenwriter, George Worthing Yates, also wrote several more sci-fi films after *Them!*–including *It Came From Beneath the Sea* (1955), *Earth vs. The Flying Saucers* (1956), *The Amazing Colossal Man* (1957), *Earth vs. The Spider* (1958) and *Frankenstein 1970* (1958).

Leonard Nimoy has a small role as an Air Force officer.

Actor James Whitmore (5'8") wore lifts to make up for some of the height difference of the towering James Arness (who is 6'7").

Edmund Gwenn (who plays Dr. Harold Bedford) also played Santa Claus in the 1934 film, *The Miracle on 34th Street.*

## TARANTULA (1955)

*"Bullets Can't Stop It! Dynamite Can't Kill It!"*

Director – Jack Arnold

Writer(s) – Robert M. Fresco / Martin Berkeley (from a story by Jack Arnold)

Starring – John Agar / Mara Corday / Leo G. Carroll / Ross Elliot / Raymond Bailey

Distributor – Universal Distributors

Released - Dec. 14, 1955

*Story:*

Called in to view a dead body with a deformed face, Dr. Matt Hastings (John Agar) can find nothing is his experience to explain it. He soon learns that a local scientist, Dr. Gerald Deemer (Leo. G. Carroll) had signed the death certificate—as the man was a colleague.

He meets the man at his laboratory outside of town and learns that the scientist is attempting to create "super-foods" for the ever-growing human population. He is using an atomic isotope and testing it on various animals and vegetables. Deemer claims that his colleague, Jacobs, had injected himself with the experimental nutrient—which caused his disfigurement and eventual death. He fails to tell Hastings about the other assistant, Lund, who was also injected. After Hastings departs, Lund returns attacks Deemer and injects the scientist with the nutrient. During the confrontation, some of the cases and cages are damaged and the tarantula—now the size of a dog—escapes into the desert, where it continues to grow.

A new lab assistant, Stephanie Clayton (Mara Corday) arrives the following day and, through as twist of fate, ends up receiving a ride from Dr, Hastings—who is returning to see Dr. Deemer again. When they arrive, they find the lab destroyed and Deemer tells them all the animals died in the fire (though the audience sees one escape—a dog-sized tarantula). Stephanie stays at Deemer's home and proves to be a very capable assistant, even though she worries about Deemer's health—as his face seems to be melting and his mood has become antagonistic.

In several interludes, we get to see the tarantula—now as big as a house—attacking and eating livestock and people (though we don't see the actual killing, it is certainly implied). Dr. Hastings tries to figure out what is happening, especially when a large pool of white liquid is found on the farm of the missing farmer and animals. The liquid turns out to be spider venom. He then tries to convince law enforcement involved to find and kill the creature.

That night, the tarantula returns to the Deemer home, and after looking into Stephanie's window (in a very cool close-up of the spider's face), the spider destroys the house—killing Dr. Deemer. Stephanie escapes with the help of the newly arrived Hastings.

The next day finds the giant spider heading towards town. Law enforcement tries bullets and dynamite, in an attempt to destroy the creature—but fail. As the tarantula seems unstoppable and appears at the edge of town, several fighter jets arrive, and using napalm, finally destroys it.

This wonderful entry into the "big bug" films is my personal favorite. The effects, using a live tarantula, are impressive for the time. The make-up effects for Dr. Deemer's transformation (done by Bud Westmore) are superb. Many of the scenes are creepy—especially the nighttime scenes—and are convincing, even with the limitations of matte special effects.

## Cool Stuff:

Clint Eastwood has a small, uncredited role as the Air Force squadron leader.

A live tarantula was used for the film. To make it move in the direction they needed, small air jets were used to persuade the spider to do so.

The gigantic two-eyed tarantula (we all know spiders have eight eyes, don't we?) seen on the movie posters, only makes an appearance in the film for extreme close-ups—like outside Mara Corday's window. It was a beautiful miniature that was to be utilized before filmmakers decided to go with a live spider.

John Agar is a veteran of film—many of which were classic horror/sci-fi films—having appeared in such films as, *The Mole People* (1956), *Attack of the Puppet People* (1958) and *Invisible Invaders* (1959).

Raymond Bailey (who plays Townsend) is most well-known as Mr. Drysdale—on the popular TV series, *The Beverly Hillbillies* (1962-71).

Director Jack Arnold claimed that they decided to make the film because people are, generally, afraid of spiders.

Look closely and you'll a giant tarantula (which many claim is a reference/homage), in one of the containment cubes, in the film *The Cabin in the Woods* (2012).

## The DEADLY MANTIS (1957)

*"A Thousand Tons of Horror! From A Million Years Ago..."*

Director – Nathan Juran

Writer(s) – Martin Berkeley / William Alland

Starring – Craig Stevens / William Hooper / Alix Talton / Pat Conway

Distributor – Universal International

Released - May 26, 1957

### Story:

After a volcano explodes, causing the polar ice caps to shift, a giant praying mantis awakens from his icy cage. Some time later, a military station (named red

Eagle Station) in northern Canada loses contact with one of their outposts. Colonel Joe Parkman (Craig Stevens) heads there to investigate—only to find the men missing and the station destroyed. Radar detects something in the sky and Parkman sends out fighter jets, and one of the jets falls from the sky after it is attacked.

Searching the wreckage, they find a strange object. Parkman takes the object to air command in Colorado, where a professor, Anton Gunther (Florenz Ames) and they determine that it is a leg from a giant praying mantis.

Paleontologist, Ned Jackson (William Hooper) and a female reporter, Marge Blaine (Alix Talton) arrive at Red Eagle One where they are attacked by the giant mantis. Gunfire and flame-throwers have no effect on it. But, when planes arrive, the mantis takes to the air and disappears. Fortunately, Ned and Marge escape and they soon find out that the mantis has just attacked a boat. Later, it also attacks a train then makes its way to Washington, D.C.—where it is seen onto of the Washington Monument.

Parkman flies his fighter jet straight into the creature and wounding it—though Parkman safely parachutes out. The mantis topples from the monument but manages to crawl into the Manhattan Tunnel. The tunnel is sealed off, and Ford—accompanied by a team of soldiers—confront the giant mantis at one entrance, forcing it forward to the other end of the tunnel, where Parkman and a special unit wait for it, armed with guns and chemical bombs. It continues to move forward and after the first two bombs fail to stop it, they begin to wonder if anything can. But, Parkman stands firm, and as the creature nears the tunnel entrance, he throws the final bomb—finally killing the giant mantis.

It ends with a trope that will become an industry standard—the dead creature moves, making them think it still lives. But, fortunately, it is merely a reflex.

A competent entry into the atomic big bug films, though it lacks the passion of its predecessors—*Them!* and *Tarantula.* Stock footage—the scene showing Eskimos escaping from the mantis is, actually, footage from the film, *S.O.S. Eisberg* (1933)—diminishes the impact. The mantis is a very cool creature to see—especially when it's in the tunnel. It is a fun film to watch, and was a huge success for Universal, but does not hold up as well as the previous films in this particular niche, though die-hard "killer bug" enthusiasts (like myself) will still enjoy it.

### *Cool Stuff:*

Director, Nathan Juran, worked on many sci-fi films—including *Attack of the 50 Foot Woman* (1958), *The 7th Voyage of Sinbad* (1958) and *First Men in the Moon* (1964). He also directed numerous episodes of such 1960's sci-fi TV series as—*Voyage to the Bottom of the Sea* (1964), *The Time Tunnel* (1966-67) and *Lost in Space* (1965-68).

William Hooper also appeared in the sci-fi film, *20 Million Miles to Earth* (1958), but is probably best known as Detective Paul Drake on the long-running TV series—*Perry Mason* (1957-66).

Phil Harvey also appeared in *The Monolith Monsters* (1957) and *Monster on Campus* (1958)

Craig Stevens is best known for his role as the star of the TV series, *Peter Gunn* (1958-61) and the film, *Gunn* (1967).

The "Manhattan Tunnel", where the mantis meets his doom, does not exist.

The Ground Observer Corps mentioned in the film were a real group of citizens who helped identify aircraft—until 1959.

Though the mantis makes a roaring sound in the film, real mantis aren't able to make any vocal sounds.

## MONSTER FROM GREEN HELL (1957)

*"The Mammoth Monster That Terrified the Earth!"*

Director – Kenneth G. Crane

Writer(s) – Endre Bohem / Louis Vittes

Starring – Jim Davis / Barbara Turner / Robert E. Griffin

Distributor – Distributors Corporation of America

Released – May 17, 1957

*Story*:

After an experiment—testing the effects of space radiation on animals—goes wrong, scientists travel to Africa to find a missing rocket.

After arriving in the jungle, they begin hearing tales of monsters. Soon after, they encounter giant green and irradiated wasps. It becomes a race against time as the scientists must find a way to destroy the creatures before they spread across the world and destroy mankind.

*Cool Stuff:*

Jim Davis went on to appear in a variety of movies and TV series. His most well-known role was as Jock Ewing on *Dallas* (1978-91).

The film contains stock footage from an earlier film, *Stanley and Livingstone* (1939).

A series of Remco Toys from the 1960s featured one called Horrible Hamilton—which is based on the giant wasps from the film.

The film was originally shot in black and white, but later VHS editions had some scenes that were shot in Technicolor.

## THE BEGINNING OF THE END (1957)

*"New Thrills! New Shocks! New Terror!"*

Director – Bert I. Gordon

Writer(s) – Fred Freiberger / Lester Gorn

Starring – Peter Graves / Peggie Castle / Richard Benedict / Morris Ankrum /

Distributor – Republic Pictures

Released – June 28, 1957

*Story*:

A journalist investigates sightings of giant grasshoppers that escaped from an experimental farm in Illinois. She teams up with an agricultural scientist and help the military battle the monsters as they head to Chicago—looking for human flesh.

*Cool Stuff*:

Peter Graves appeared in many Horror/Sci-Fi films in his long career. He can be found in such classics as *Red Planet Mars* (1952), *Killers From Space* (1954), and *It Conquered the World* (1956). He was also a regular on the TV series, *Mission Impossible* (1967-73).

There were 200 live grasshoppers used in the film, but because they are notorious cannibals only a dozen remained once filming ended.

The boom mic's shadow can be seen in several shots.

**THE BLACK SCORPION (1957)**

*"The hideous inhuman being that defied every law of nature. "*

Director – Edward Ludwig

Writer(s) – Robert Blees / David Duncan

Starring – Richard Denning / Mara Corday / Carlos Rivas

Distributor – Warner Bros.

Release Date - Oct.11, 1957.

## *Story:*

After an earthquake causes a volcano to appear in Mexico, two geologists—Dr. Hank Scott (Richard Dennings) and Dr. Arturo Ramos (Carlos Rivas) travel there to study the extraordinary phenomenon. Before they reach the nearby village, they find a house and police car, both destroyed, as well as a policeman's dead body and an infant that is still alive. Racing to the village with the infant, where they are met by a priest, Father Delgado (Pedro Galvan), who informs them that there have been many horrific events since the earthquake—missing people, livestock mutilations, damaged homes, and strange sounds in the night. He suggests that leave but the two geologists forge ahead.

The Mexican Army arrives to aid the village. Meanwhile, Dr. Scott falls a rancher –Teresa Alvarez (Mara Corday)—just before the volcano erupts again, unleashing a next of giant scorpions on the village. The army fires on them, but to no avail, and the creatures return to their lair—which turns out to be home to giant spiders and worms, as well. After calling in an entomologist—Dr. Valasco (Carlos Muzquiz)—they track the creatures back to their lair and seal of the entrance.

Unfortunately, several of the scorpions escape and attack a train, then begin to fight each other. The largest eventually kills the others and makes its way towards Mexico City. Our hero doctors devise a plan to lure the creature to a stadium by using a truck full of meat to attract it. Once there, the military hits it with a barrage of weapons—which proves ineffective. Just when it seems that the scorpion is unbeatable, Dr. Scott attaches an electrical cable to a makeshift spear and shoots it down the creature's throat, eventually electrocuting it to death—and saving the day.

One of the more visually terrifying and convincing of the killer bug films—you get to people getting killed by the creatures—thanks to the quality work of Willis O'Brien and Pete Peterson, who, even though they were working under time constraints and on a limited budget, produced some incredible stop-motion work. A great choice for "big bug" film fans—and connoisseurs of stop-motion creature work—that's layered with a competent story and some realistic terror.

*Cool Stuff:*

The scorpion sound is the same tree frog singing we heard in *Them!*

Willis O'Brien (of King Kong fame) and Pete Peterson did the stop-motion effects.

The brief scene where the trapdoor spider attacks Juanito is the same spider that was deleted from King Kong (1933).

Richard Denning also starred in such sci-fi/horror films as *Creature from the Black Lagoon*, *Creature with the Atom Brain*, and *Day the World Ended*.

Mara Corday also starred in *Tarantula* (1955), *The Black Scorpion* (1957), and *The Giant Claw* (1957).

When the scorpion attacks the train, the Lionel Corporation logo can be seen (if you look real close), giving away the fact it was an actual miniature.

## THE FLY (1958)

*"Once it was human—even as you and I!"*

Director – Kurt Newman

Writer(s) – James Clavell (based on the story by George Langelaan)

Starring – David Hedison / Patricia Owens / Vincent Price

Distributor – 20th Century Fox

Released – Aug. 29, 1958

## Story:

*The Fly* doesn't give us the atomic giants of previous films like *Them!, Tarantula* and *Black Scorpion*—but science is still at its core.

Helene Delambre (Patricia Owens) confesses to the murder of her husband—Andre Delambre (David Hedison)—when he is found dead, after being crushed in a hydraulic press. When questioned about the death, we relive her story in a flashback.

Andre is a scientist, working on a transporter device (the disintegrator-integrator). He tests it—first on inanimate objects, then on, living creatures. He then tests it on the family cat and a guinea pig. Confident he has perfected the experiment, he builds a larger device and tests it on himself. Unknown to Andre, a fly has entered the chamber with him, and when he activates the device, his life is changed forever.

When Helene, worried that she has not seen him for several days, goes down to the lab, she finds Andre wearing a black hood on his head–and his left arm is also covered in a large black cloth. Unable to speak, he writes down that he used the transporter on himself—but a fly was in the device and their atoms have mixed. When she removes the hood—seeking proof—she finds his human head is now that of a fly. Naturally, she screams and we get to see her through his eyes–the eyes of a fly.

He informs her that he must find the fly—that now has a tiny human head and arm—and they must re-enter the transporter and hope to reverse the mistake, because his mind and will are becoming less human, and more like a fly. She frantically searches for the fly, but without success. With what little will remained in him, he destroys his lab, burns his notes and convinces Helene to stop him. Setting the hydraulic press, he has Helene push the button—which she does twice—once for the head, once for the arm.

The police, of course, think she is insane and are convinced she is guilty of Andre's murder. Just as she is about to be taken to jail, her son, Phillippe (Charles Herbert) tells his uncle, Francois (Vincent Price) that he has found a strange-looking fly in a spider web. Francois convinces Inspector Charas (Herbert Marshall) to come see the fly for himself. As they watch the creature—a fly with a human head and arm—struggle in the web, crying out "Help me, help me" as the spider draws closer, the Inspector–now shocked and disgusted–picks up a rock and smashes the tiny creatures.

Francois wonders if the Inspector could now be guilty of murder—for killing a fly with human body parts. Knowing that no one will believe the truth, the Inspector lies about what actually happened, and Helene is free from guilt. The family is allowed to go back to their lives.

One of the best "killer bug" films, *The Fly* succeeds on many levels. The actors are superb (even though Price and Herbert struggled to keep a straight face for the fly/human stuck in the web scene—where an animatronic figure is used). Hedison is wonderful as the scientist Delambre, his mannerism and actions while in the Fly makeup is satisfyingly realized. Patricia Owens projects a convincing image of the concerned, yet frightened and determined wife. The Fly makeup, created by Ben Nye, is still one of the best facial makeup creatures in Horror/Monster cinema. The story is very satisfyingly original and executed (even though the ending was changed to appear more upbeat).

Though some of the effects don't hold up after all these years, the film is still one of high quality and, rightfully, considered a classic in the genre. Every monster or "killer bug" film fan should have this in their library.

### *Cool Stuff:*

David Hedison is truly the man beneath the Fly makeup. No stuntman or stand-in was used—which happens all too often because the actors want their face on-screen.

The original story (written by George Langelaan), was first published in Playboy—in their June 1957 issue.

The Distributor changed the ending of the film from the short story—to give it a happy ending (Helene commits suicide in the short story).

James Clavell (who adapted Langelaan's story), went on to become a highly successful novelist—with such bestsellers as, *Shogun, Taipan* and *Noble House*.

Makeup man, Ben Nye, has a long and successful career. His works can be found in such diverse films as *Gone with the Wind* (1939), *Dr. Doolittle* (1967), and *Planet of the Apes* (1968).

Patricia Owens—who has a genuine fear of insects—didn't get to see the Fly makeup until Hedison appeared in it. Her on-screen reaction is laced with some actual fear.

Sadly, Director Kurt Newman died just a month after the premiere of the film—so he never got to see it become the most successful film of his career.

## (EARTH vs.) THE SPIDER (1958)

*"Bullets Won't Kill It! Flames Can't Hurt It! Nothing Can Stop It!"*

Director – Bert I. Gordon

Writer(s) – Laszlo Gorog / George Worthing Yates / Bert I. Gordon

Starring – Ed Kemmer / June Kenney / Gene Roth / Eugene Persson

Distributor – American International Pictures (AIP)

Release Date – Release Sept. 1, 1958

*Story:*

When her father fails to return home one night, Carol Flynn (June Kenney) and her boyfriend, Mike Simpson (Eugene Persson) go looking for him—and find his crashed truck, but nobody. They end up in a cave and fall into a giant spider web. A giant tarantula appears, but the couple manages to escape. They go to Sheriff Cagle (Gene Roth), who doesn't believe a word the young couple is claiming but does go to the cave—accompanied by science teacher, Mr. Kingman (Ed Kemmer), to investigate—where they find the old man's body, which has been drained dry. They encounter the spider, and soon return with a massive amount of DDT, which kills the spider—or so they think.

They take the spider to the high school gymnasium so that Mr. Kingman can study it. Unfortunately, a group of teenagers decides to use the gym to play some rock n' roll. The spider wakes and the teens escape the gym—the spider following behind them. The creature attacks Kingman's home (where his wife and infant are), but Kingman rams it was his car. It leaves but kills a handful of people on its way back to its home in the cave.

The teenage couple (Carol and Mike)—are in the cave looking for her father's bracelet, when the spider returns—trapping them on a ledge. Kingman and Sheriff Cagle arrive with dynamite—hoping to seal the spider in—but must save the teen couple first. Kingman places some electrodes on the web and when the giant spider crawls on the web—it is electrocuted and falls to its death onto some stalagmites.

The weakest entry of the 50's "big bug" films, it fails on many levels—special effects that seem lazy and uninspired, film errors (especially some obvious matte shots), acting that seems phoned-in, and a very poor story—makes this film forgettable. Riding the "teenage movie" train that was becoming popular at the time, the film seems more concerned with the teenagers (and their music, cars, romance) than the spider. Watch this one only if you are a die-hard fan. Otherwise, this is one you can avoid without too much sadness.

*Cool Stuff:*

Bert I. Gordon directed many fun (though not great) Sci-Fi/Horror films with a "giant" theme—*The Amazing Colossal Man* (1957), *Attack of the Puppet People* (1958), *Village of the Giants* (1965), *Food of the Gods* (1976), and *Empire of the Ants* (1977).

The giant spider "web" was made of rope (which was used in the film–even though Tarantulas don't spin webs). One of its many mistakes.

Producers decided to market the film under the title *The Spider* after the success of *The Fly* (1958)— which was released earlier in the year. The film, itself, still retains the title *Earth vs. The Spider*.

## RETURN OF THE FLY (1965)

*"Out of the World of Atomic Mutation It Rises – With the Dread Curse of the father Upon It!"*

Director – Edward Bernds

Writer(s) – Edward Bernds (based on the short story by George Langelaan

Starring – Vincent Price / Brett Halsey / David Frankham / Danielle De Metz

Distributor – 20th Century Fox

Released - July 1959

### Story:

15 years after the death of his father, Phillipe Delambre seeks to perfect the telepod that his father created—and which killed him.

When his uncle Francois (Vincent Price) refuses to help support the experiments, Phillipe hires Alan Hinds—who turns out to be an industrial spy. When confronted, Hinds (aka Ronald Holmes) knocks Phillip out and puts him in the telepod, then throws a fly into the mix, which produces a Phillipefly (Phillipe with a fly head, arm and leg) as well as fly with Phillipe's head, arm and leg.

The now mutated "Phillipefly" chases and kills Hinds. After he returns home, an inspector manages to capture him and the mutated fly. After putting them into the telepod, Phillipe is returned to normal.

### Cool Stuff:

Vincent Price was the only actor who was also in the original film.

The studio wanted to use the set pieces from the previous film and wrote the screenplay to make use of them.

The film was released on a double bill—with *The Alligator People* (1959).

The director of the original *The Fly* (1958), Kurt Neumann, died before production began on the sequel.

Though the previous film was shot in color, budgetary reasons was likely the reason this film was shot in black-and-white.

Though it has not been definitively verified, the walking stick used by Ronald Holmes is believed to be Larry Talbot's wolf's head cane *from The Wolfman* (1941)—that's been painted white.

## ATTACK OF THE GIANT LEECHES (1959)

*"Crawling Horror...Rising From The Depths Of Hell...To Kill And Conquer!"*

Director – Bernard L. Kowalski

Writer(s) – Leo Gordon

Starring – Ken Clark / Yvette Vickers / Jan Shepard

Studio – A.I.P.

Released – Oct. 1959

*Story:*

When trappers, in the Florida Everglades, begin disappearing, a game warden's investigation leads him to the killers—giant leeches in the swamps.

*Cool Stuff:*

Writer, Leo Gordon, was also an actor—appearing in a variety of films/TV shows (primarily as a character actor). He can be found in *Gunsmoke* (1956-74), The Rockford Files (1978-79), and *The Garbage Pail Kids Movie* (1987).

Star, Yvette Vickers helped promote the film by appearing in Playboy magazine. She also appeared in *Attack of the 50 Foot Woman* (1958).

The film's score was not original, it was the same score used in *Night of the Blood Beast* (1958).

The giant "leeches" were just actors wearing black plastic suits—not much different from a trash bag—with suckers sewn onto them.

## HORRORS OF SPIDER ISLAND (aka BODY IN THE WEB) (1960)

*"Transformed into The World's Most Hideous Monster"*

Director – Jaimie Nolan (Fritz Bottger)

Writer(s) – Fritz Bottger / Eldon Howard / Albert G. Miller

Starring – Harald Maresch / Helga Franck

Distributor – Pacemaker Pictures / Rapid-Film Intercontinental (USA)

Released – Apr. 1960 (Germany) / March 1962 (USA)

*Story:*

Survivors of a plane crash battle spiders. The spider bites also turn its victims into giant mutated spider people.

*Cool Stuff:*

The film was originally titled *It's Hot in Paradise* (in 1962) as an Adult film—because it contained nudity. In 1965, the nude scenes were removed, and it was renamed *Horrors of Spider Island.*

Alexander D'Arcy also appeared in *Blood of Dracula's Castle* (1969).

## MOTHRA (1961)

*"Mightiest Monster in All Creation. Ravishing A Universe for Love."*

Director – Ishiro Honda

Writer – Shinichi Tanaka

Starring – Frankie Sakai / Kyoko Kagawa / Hiroshi Koizumi / Robert Dunham

Distributor – Toho (Japan) / Columbia (USA)

Released – July 30, 1961 (Japan) / May 10, 1962 (USA)

*Story:*

A ship runs aground on Infant Island—where, in years past, it was used for atomic tests. When a rescue party arrives, they find four survivors safe and sound—seemingly healthy from drinking a special juice provided by the islanders. Until then, the island was thought to be uninhabited. This incident attracts a reporter named Zenichiro Fukuda (Frankie Sakai) and photographer Michi Hanamura (Kyoko Kagawa), who

The news forced the Rolisician Embassy (who were responsible for the previous atomic tests) to work with the Japanese government to explore the island. A group of individuals from various areas of expertise are gathered to undertake an expedition—led by entrepreneur Clark Nelson (Jerry Itou).

While at the island, they discover two women, (both 12-inches tall,), who want nothing more than to have their island be free of further atomic tests. The team promises them there will be no more tests and leave the island in peace.

But, Nelson returns with his own group and abducts the tiny women. He brings them to Tokyo and uses them as a sideshow attraction. Our intrepid reporters accuse Nelson of keeping the women against their will—and a legal battle ensues.

Meanwhile, back on Infant Island, the natives are praying to a giant egg. Eventually, the egg hatches and giant caterpillar appears and heads across the sea towards Tokyo. It cocoons against a tower, then transforms into the giant moth we know as Mothra— where it battles the Japanese army, all while laying waste to the city. The reporters manage to rescue the women and deliver them to Mothra, where they are carried back to Infant Island.

*Mothra* would go on to become one of the most popular kaiju characters to come out of Toho Distributors (second only to Godzilla). She would appear with Godzilla in 7 films and get her own trilogy in the 1990s.

### *Cool Stuff:*

The U.S. version has a long list of credits—which doesn't include the top 3 stars. And the villain of the film (Jerry Ito) is listed as Jelly Ito. The film was released in the U.S. as part of a double bill. The other film—*The Three Stooges In Orbit* (1962).

The U.S. version is 10 minutes shorter than the Japanese version.

The island that Mothra is from is called Infant Island, but in the U.S. version, it's called Beirut. It is later changed back to Infant Island in Mothra's other film appearances.

An origin story for Mothra and the fairies was proposed but was scrapped because of its length.

Director, Ishiro Honda, directed many of Toho's Daikaiju films—the original *Godzilla* (1954) film, as well as, *King Kong vs. Godzilla* (1962), *War of the Gargantuas* (1966), *Destroy All Monsters* (1968), and *Terror of Mechagodzilla* (1975).

The fairies—twins, Emi & Yumi Ito—were a successful music duo, often covering European hits for the Japanese audience.

The film is based on a serialized novel titled—The Luminous Fairies and Mothra—that appeared in Weekly Asahi.

## CURSE OF THE FLY (1965)

"

Director – Don Sharp

Writer(s) – Harry Spalding

Starring – Brian Donlevy / Carole Gray / George Baker / Michael Graham

Distributor – 20th Century Fox

Released – May 1965

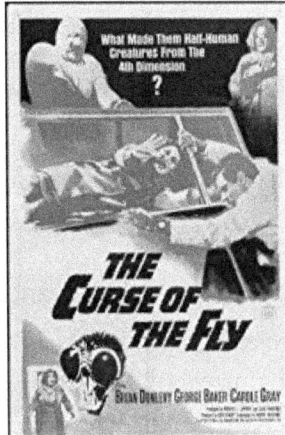

*Story:*

Andre Delambre's sons and grandsons continue his telepod experiments, resulting in a new set of mutations—minus actual flies this time.

*Cool Stuff:*

Vincent Price was unable to return for this installment, as he was under contract with AIP.

Phillipe, the son from the previous film, is absent from the storyline.

The film was a box office disappointment—unlike the previous films.

Although the first two films were available on video years later, this film did not receive a video release until 2007—as part of a box set with *The Fly* (1958) and *Return of the Fly* (1959).

## THE DEADLY BEES (1967)

*"Hives of Horror!"*

Director – Freddie Francis

Writer(s) – Robert Bloch / Anthony Marriot / based on the novel by Gerald Heard

Distributor – Amicus Productions / Paramount Pictures

Released – 1966 (UK) / May 19, 1967 (USA)

### Story:

A singer takes a break from her career and visits a small island resort to relax. Soon, she and other residents must fight for their lives when they are attacked by a swarm of deadly bees.

_Cool Stuff:_

The film is loosely based on the novel, _A Taste of Honey_ by H.F. Heard. It was published in 1941.

The screenplay was co-written by Robert Bloch (author of _Psycho_), but later rewritten by Anthony Marriott—who took the story further away from the original novel.

Director Freddie Francis helmed many genre films in his career. _The Evil of Frankenstein_ (1964), _Dracula Has Risen From the Grave_ (1968), _Tales From the Crypt_ (1972), and _Trog_ (1970). He directed 8 Peter Cushing films.

Freddie Francis was also a renowned cinematographer, with such films as _The Elephant Man_ (1980), _Cape Fear_ (1991), and _Glory_ (1989) for which he won an Academy Award.

Guitarist, Ron Wood plays is one of the members of the onscreen band, The Birds. This was before he became a member of one of the greatest rock bands of all time—The Rolling Stones.

Susanna Leigh also appeared in _The Lost Continent_ (1968) and _Lust for the Vampire_ (1971).

Frank Finlay-whose career spans over 50 years—also appeared in _Lifeforce_ (1985) and as Jacob Marley in the TV movie version of _A Christmas Carol_ (1984).

## WAR OF THE INSECTS (aka GENOCIDE) (1968)

Director – Kazui Nihonmastsu (as Norman Cooper)

Writer(s) – Susumu Takaku / Kingen Amada

Starring – Yusuke Kawazu / Keisuke Sonoi

Distributor – Shochiku

Released – November 1968 (Japan) / 1969 (USA)

_Story:_

Experiments on poisonous insects and the search for an H-Bomb (which has been accidently dropped on a Japanese island), lead to earth's insect population to begin attacking the human race—plunging the world into chaos.

*Cool Stuff:*

Kazui Nihonmatsu also directed *The X from Outer Space* (1967).

Cinematographer, Shizuo Hirase also worked on *The X from Outer Space* (1967) and *Goke, Body Snatcher from Hell* (1968).

Yusuke Kawazu also appeard in *Godzilla vs Mechagodzilla II* (1993) and *Gamera 2: Attack of the Legion* (1996).

Kathy Horan appeared in *The Green Slime* (1968).

It was released on a double-bill with *The Living Skeleton*.

This was the final film produced by Shochiku Eiga.

## THE HELLSTROM CHRONICLE (1971)

*"Science Fiction? No. Science Fact."*

Director – Ed Spiegel / Walon Green

Writer(s) – David Seltzer

Starring – Lawrence Pressman

Distributor – Cinema 5

Released – June 28, 1971

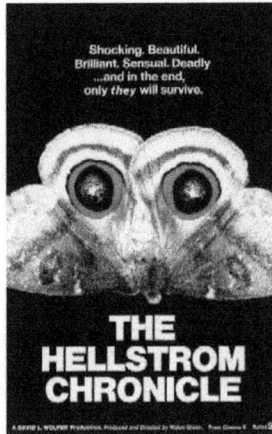

## Story:

Narrated by Dr. Hellstrom (Lawrence Pressman), the film uses elements of horror/science fiction—combined with the current scientific evidence available at the time—to create a film that speculates what could happen if insects decided to conquer the world.

Beautiful cinematography, stop motion effects, and brief clips from various horror/scfi-fi films give it a cinematic feel similar to many of the other films in this book.

## Cool Stuff:

The film won an Academy Award and a BAFTA for Best Documentary Feature in 1972.

David Wolper also produced *Willy Wonka and the Chocolate Factory* (1971)—which played on a double-bill with the film.

Director Walon Green can be seen in *Willy Wonka and the Chocolate Factory's* tunnel scene. He is the face on the wall having a centipede crawling over it.

Lawrence Pressman is probably best known for his portrayal of Dr. Benjamin Canfield *on Doogie Howser M.D.* (1989-93).

Frank Herbert (of Dune fame) used the film as inspiration for his 1973 novel, Hellstrom's Hive.

The film used two entomologist, from the Los Angeles County Museum of Natural History, as technical advisors—Roy Snelling and Charles Hogue.

The film was purposely promoted as a science fiction film with trailers to match.

One particular time-lapse scene shows the depressingly short 17-hour life-cycle of the May Fly—in just a few minutes.

David Seltzer was nominated for Original Screenplay for the Writer's Guild of America. He is best known as the writer of the *Omen* films—for which he also wrote the novelizations.

Even though Dr. Nils Hellstrom (M.S., Ph.D according to the end credits) is fictional, he has been quoted in contemporary discussions. But, even though he is fictional, his comments are not. They were statements made by the entomologists mentioned above.

## THE KILLER BEES (1974)

*"She controls the bees. They'll kill for her—and die for her."*

Director – Curtis Harrington

Writer(s) – John & Joyce Corrington

Starring – Kate Jackson / Edward Albert / Gloria Swanson

Distributor – ABC

Released – Feb. 26, 1974

### Story:

A woman runs a successful wine business and also controls a swarm of killer bees—with the power of her mind.

### Cool Stuff:

Kate Jackson is best known for her role as Sabrina Duncan on the TV series, *Charlie's Angels* (1976-79).

Gloria Swanson—who began her acting career in 1914--was impressive during filming. She wore a corset to straighten her back and allowed the bees to crawl on her without complaint. She was 74 during filming. It was her penultimate film. Her final film, *Airport 1975*, was released the same year.

Edward Albert appeared in many TV shows and films, including Galaxy of Terror (1981), The House Where Evil Dwells (1982), and *Power Rangers Time Force* (2001), as Mr. Collins.

Roger Davis played two separate characters on the TV series, *Dark Shadows* (1968-70), and played Andromus on *Galactica 1980*.

Bettie Davis was originally picked for the film, but because she is allergic to bee stings, her doctor nixed that idea.

Nearly 700,000 bees were used in the film.

### PHASE IV (1974)

*"Adapt or Die"*

Director – Saul Bass

Written – Mayo Simon

Starring – Michael Murphy / Nigel Davenport / Lynne Frederick

Distributor – Paramount Pictures

Released – September 1974

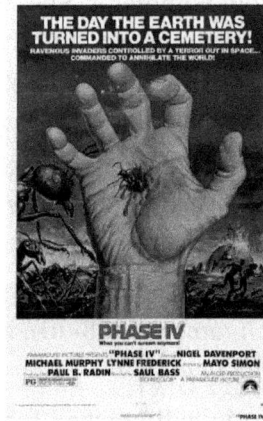

## Story:

After an unknown cosmic event—ants have evolved and have begun doing "things that ants don't do", says James Lesko (Michael Murphy)—who narrates portions of the opening. Ernest Hubbs (Nigel Davenport) had already been studying the phenomenon, even when the rest of the world had already forgotten about the event. We see several minutes of the ants acting as a hive mind and building things with geometrical shapes—as well as killing and consuming a spider.

Hubbs invites Lesko to join him in his studies—and in the Arizona desert, they investigate a series of strange towers and geometric crop circles. The local residents are asked to evacuate – leaving only one family. The scientists are pressured to speed things up by the government—who is funding the project—so they blow up the towers in hopes of getting a reaction. That night the ants attack the remaining family's farm—killing their horse and destroying their home. They head for the lab but crash the truck after ants attack them. Climbing from the truck, they continue to walk to the lab. Unaware of what's going on outside, Hubbs and Lesko, who are studying the signals and believe the insects are sending out commands, hear an explosion outside—which turns out to be their own vehicle. Hubbs sprays chemicals to teach the ants a lesson. They go out the next morning to find the family is dead, from the chemical spray—except for the daughter, Kendra (Lynne Frederick), who was hiding in the cellar.

Later that night, Kendra, in a fit of anger, destroys some lab equipment, which allows the ants to escape. Hubbs is bitten, but the trio escapes the room and fumigates it—killing the specimens. The scene switches to show us the ants dragging a piece of the chemical through one of their tunnels. It dies, but another ant comes along and continues to drag it forward—followed by another, then another, until the chemical finally makes its way to the queen, who ingests it.

The next morning, the trio wakes to find there are new towers surrounded them—they are smaller and have been built-in a perfect circle around the dome. When the sun hits the top of the towers, is heats up the dome—nearly baking our trio inside. They use sound to destroy the new towers. Meanwhile, ants have gotten into the computers and begin chewing on the wires—where a praying mantis is waiting. But, a newer generation of ants—now immune to the chemicals, kills the mantis. The ants short out the computers.

Then we get to see the ants carrying their dead underground and laying them side by side, in rows—like humans would do after a tragic event. Lesko begins to see more and more messages—mathematical ones—from the ants, then begins to send them messages in an attempt to communicate. The next morning, new towers have been built and Hubbs, in his delirium from the bite, believes that Kendra is somehow responsible for the ants knowing what they are doing. When Lesko receives a message, indicating that they ants want something (or someone) in the lab, Kendra, thinking she may be the reason—because she killed the specimens—leaves the safety of the lab and walks out into the night.

Hubbs and Lesko continue to butt heads because Hubbs now wants to destroy the ants while Lesko wants to communicate with them—as they are proving to be more intelligent as the days pass. Hubbs goes outside, determined to destroy the colony. Instead, he falls into a deep, square pit. Before Lesko can rescue Hubbs, ants pour out of tunnels in the pit and begin to consume him. Lesko then realizes that the ants intend to spread out—where they will eventually become unstoppable.

In a last-ditch effort, Lesko (who narrates the final moments) takes a canister of poison, sprays the area on his way to the hive. Once there, he slides down a hole, where he finds Kendra, who rises from the sand. The two embrace, and Lesko learns that the ants do not want to destroy humanity, but merge with them—and create a new, superior species. They now wait for further instructions.

Focusing more on questions of evolution, intelligence and the mind, the film moved away from the typical creature features of the past—who were, usually, accidents of science—and who sought our destruction. It has some of that great psychedelic music and sounds effects—as well as great photographic work with the ants in their underground chambers. Though very outdated, it is a nostalgic representation of early 1970's computer technology. It was a very under-appreciated and intelligent thriller that has become a cult classic over the years—even though it was a box-office failure during its original release. One of my favorite entries in the "killer bug" genre.

## *Cool Stuff:*

The film was the only feature-length film directed by Saul Bass, who claims the Distributor messed with the film after he finished production.

Bass was a well-known graphic designer who designed many movie posters and title sequences. He also created several popular logos—the Bell System (1969), United Airlines tulip (1974) and the AT&T globe (1983).

Nigel Davenport started in many horror/thriller/sci-fi films over his long career—*Peeping Tom* (1960), *The Picture of Dorian Grey* (1973), *Dracula* (1973) and *The Island of Dr. Moreau* (1977).

Michael Murphy is one of those actors that make you say, "I know that guy". A character actor, he has appeared in dozens and TV shows (usually as a villain). His roles include—*Shocker* (1989), *Batman Returns* (1992) and *X-Men: The Last Stand* (2006).

Lynne Frederick—who tragically died at age 39—also appeared the classic Hammer film, *Vampire Circus* (1972), as well as *Schizo* (1976) and *Voyage of the Damned* (1976).

The actual title of the film does not appear until closer to the end, as it goes through the first 3 Phases throughout.

It is the first film to feature a geometric crop circle (2 years before modern reports started appearing in the U.K.). The crop circle in the film is a creation of the ants.

Wildlife photographer, Ken Middleham, shot the insect sequences—and was also the photographer for the *Hellstrom Chronicle* documentary.

The ant queens seen in the film are actually a species of wasp.

Barry N. Malzberg (a popular science fiction writer) wrote the novelization.

It is available on DVD but lacks any special features, which is disappointing, as the trailer for the film actually shows the ending scene that was removed from the final cut.

# BUG (1975)

*"Out of the Worst Nightmare!"*

Director – Jeannot Szwarc

Writer(s) – Thomas Page / William Castle / based on the novel *The Hephaestus Plague* by Thomas Page

Starring Bradford Dillman / Joanna Miles / Richard Gilliland / Alan Fudge

Distributor – Paramount Pictures

Released – June 17, 1975

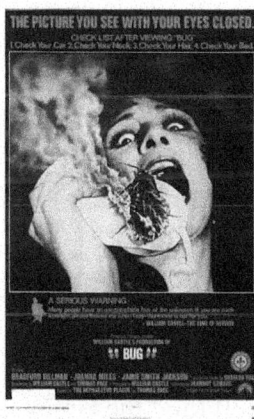

<u>Story:</u>

The film begins with an earthquake that shakes up the audience in a church. As a young couple is looking at a large hole that has opened in the ground, a truck is arriving, but suddenly bursts into flames—killing the driver and his son. We are then introduced to the film's villains, cockroaches. It seems they are responsible for the truck fire. Later that night, the husband hears strange noises outside and investigates.

Finding one of the roaches, he picks it up and it burns him—then he sees a cat burned by the bugs, as well as various areas of the yard being ignited by the bugs.

He brings one of the roaches to science teacher, James Parmiter (Bradford Dillman), who goes to the home to find more of the bugs, and soon discovers the roaches can start fires, and even eat the ash. Meanwhile strange fires are breaking out all over town. Parmiter tries to warn officials that the fires are being started by the bugs.

After his wife is killed—burned alive by the bugs— Parmiter becomes obsessed with the roaches and begins experimenting with them at the home where the hole originated. He discovers they can be killed using high atmospheric pressure and has a fellow Professor—Metbaum (Richard Gilliand)—create a portable pressure chamber. Parmiter does more extensive tests. He starts by introducing a common male cockroach to one of the sexless "firebugs". Surprisingly, the two roaches do mate. The resulting egg case grows even larger than the firebug itself. When it hatches, Parmiter even names the news species after himself (and the Greek God of fire)— Hephaetus parmitera.

As the days pass, his obsession grows. He places the "mother" is with the new species, and the young ones kill her. One evening, while Parmiter is preparing his dinner, several of the roaches escape and begin consuming a raw steak—but only as a combined unit. They escape again and climb onto Parmiter while he is sleeping—and begin draining his blood. They seem to prefer raw meat and fresh blood, as well as begin to form patterns—as if they are trying to communicate. When he awakes one night, he finds they have spelled out his name "Parmiter" on the wall. They even spell out letters he asks them to. But, when they spell "We Live", Parmiter feels they must be destroyed— perhaps feeling he has moved them too far on the evolutionary ladder—and rushes out of the house to get another pressure chamber.

While he is gone, a friend visits, but is killed by the roaches, while the other roaches remove the newest egg sacks and take them down the hole in the ground from whence they came. When Parmiter finally discovers the body—then hears strange, loud noises coming from the hole—and sees the firebugs have now developed the ability to fly. They begin attacking Parmiter, who flees out the door—in flames—and falls into the hole. The roaches follow after him, and the hole collapses behind them.

Were the firebugs creatures from Hell? Were they seeking to merge with mankind and become a new species? Were they our punishment for trying to play God? Were they a lost species that Parmiter (perhaps becoming a mad scientist in the film) turns into a blight on mankind—his own Frankenstein monster? Were they punishment for our arrogance? You decide.

Either way, the film is a creepy little addition to the killer bug genre. There are some truly terrifying moments—hair being ignited, flesh being burnt, etc.—especially if you hate cockroaches. As is usually the case, I recommend reading the novel, if you want a more detailed and expanded story. A must-see for killer bug fans.

### Cool Stuff:

Sadly, this was the last film William Castle worked on (as producer/writer) before his death in 1977. His is best known, to Horror fans, as director of such classics as—*House on Haunted Hill* (1959), *The Tingler* (1959), *13 Ghosts* (1960), and *Mr. Sardonicus* (1961). He was also a producer on *Rosemary's Baby* (1968).

Castle liked to use a "gimmick" for some of his films, by adding things to some theaters. In this particular case, he had brushes installed near the theater seats, which would rub against people's legs—making them think bugs were crawling on them.

Director, Jeannot Szwarc also directed many other films and TV shows, such as—*Jaws 2* (1978), *Supergirl* (1984), and *Santa Claus: The Movie* (1985). His TV work includes—*The Devil's Daughter* (1973), 19 episodes of *Night Gallery*, 14 episodes of *Smallville*, and 3 episodes of *Supernatural*.

Bradford Dillman has appeared in such genre films as—*Escape From the Planet of the Apes* (1971), *Piranha* (1978), and *Lords of the Deep* (1989).

Joanna Miles starred in *The Dark Secret of Harvest Home* (1978), and also appeared in *Star Trek: The Next Generation* (1990-91) and *Judge Dredd* (1995).

Madagascar hissing cockroaches—which were used in the film—are one of the most popular bugs to be used in film/TV, mainly because of their size.

Some of the cockroaches, used for special scenes, were the creation of Karoly Forgassy (a technical illustrator at the University of California at Riverside). The live insect sequences were the work of Ken Middleham—who was also responsible for the ant sequences in *Phase IV* (1974).

The Parmiter home, though altered for the film, was the same set that was used for the interior of The Brady Bunch home.

### The GIANT SPIDER INVASION (1975)

*"Creeping! Clawing!...Crushing!"*

Director – Bill Rebane

Writer(s) – Robert Easton / Richard L. Huff

Starring – Steve Brodie / Robert Easton / Alan Hale Jr. / Barbara Hale

Distributor – Group 1 International Distribution Organization Ltd.

Released – Oct. 24, 1975

*Story:*

After meteors fall to Earth, spiders escape from inside them—some of which grow to gigantic proportions—and are unleashed upon the local populace.

*Cool Stuff:*

The giant spider was actually a VW Beetle—with puppet legs attached.

Bill Rebane was responsible—as producer and director—of several other b-movies, such as *Monster a-Go Go* (1965), *The Alpha Incident* (1978), and *The Capture of Bigfoot* (1979).

Alan Hale Jr. is best known as The Skipper on *Gilligan's Island* (1964-67).

Leslie Parrish also appeared in many TV shows, including *The Wild Wild West* (1965-66) and *Batman* (1966-67), and *Logan's Run* (1977).

The film cost a meager $300,000 to produce.

**KISS OF THE TARANTULA (1976)**

*"So silent. So deadly. So final."*

Director – Chris Munger

Writer(s) – Daniel Cady / Warren Hamilton Jr.

Starring – Suzanna Ling / Eric Mason / Herman Wallner

Distributor – Cinema-Vu

Released – May 1976

*Story:*

A teenage girl (Susan), whose parents run a mortuary, learns of her mother's plot to kill her father. She puts a tarantula in her mother's bed, and her mother dies of a heart attack as a result. Susan then proceeds to use her pet tarantulas to exact revenge on her own tormentors at shcool

*Cool Stuff:*

The film was the first, and last, role for Suzanna Ling.

Screenwriter, Daniel Cady, also produced and/or wrote such classics as *Garden of the Dead* (1972*), Black Samson* (1974), and *Dolly Dearest* (1991).

Eric Mason also appeared in *Scream, Blacula, Scream* (1973).

## THE FOOD OF THE GODS (1976)

*"One taste is all it takes"*

Director – Bert I. Gordon

Writer(s) – Bert I. Gordon (based on the story by H.G. Wells)

Starring - Marjoe Gortner / Pamela Franklin / Ida Lupino / Ralph Meeker

Distributor – A.I.P.

Released – June 18, 1976

## Story:

On a remote island in British Columbia, a strange substance in the ground causes the farm animals to grow to huge proportions.

When a group of hunters travel to the island, they—and the residents—soon find themselves battling for their lives against giant rats, wasps and worms.

## Cool Stuff:

Based (somewhat loosely) on the story by H.G. Wells.

Marjoe Gortner also appeared in *Earthquake* (1974), *Starcrash* (1978) and *Mausoleum* (1983).

Pamela Franklin also starred in *The Legend of Hell House* (1973).

There were six mechanical rat heads and four rat costumes used in the film.

## SQUIRM (1976)

*"This was the night of the Crawling Terror!"*

Director – Jeff Lieberman

Writer(s) – Jeff Lieberman

Starring – Don Scardino / Patricia Pearcy / Jean Sullivan

Distributor – A.I.P.

Released – July 30, 1976

### Story:

A freak storm in the small town of Fly Creek, Georgia causes the power lines to fall—electrifying the ground. The electricity turns worms into mutated, flesh-eating creatures—who begin terrorizing the residents.

### Cool Stuff:

The worm's "screeching" were an electronic version created to mimic pigs in a slaughterhouse.

Though the exact number is unknown, it's estimated that over a million worms were used.

Jeff Lieberman also directed 2004's *Satan's Little Helper*.

Don Scardino went on to appear in such TV shows as *Cosby* (1997-2000), *Law & Order* (1991-2006), and *30 Rock* (2006-12).

It features some early makeup work by Rick Baker.

It was actor Roger Grimes only film role.

The film was completed in just 24 days.

## EMPIRE OF THE ANTS (1977)

*"For They Shall Inherit the Earth—Sooner Than You Think!"*

Director – Bert I. Gordon

Writer(s) – Bert I. Gordon / Jack Turley (based on a story by H.G. Wells)

Starring – Joan Collins / Robert Lansing / John Carson

Distributor – A.I.P.

Released – July 29, 1977

## Story:

Attempting to scam a group of land buyers into buying fake real estate, a con artist invites them to a small island in the Florida Everglades. Unfortunately, the group becomes trapped on the island with giant, killer ants.

## Cool Stuff:

The film is loosely based on the short story, *Empire of the Ants*, by H.G. Wells (published in 1905).

Bert I. Gordon is an icon of the genre, having directed or produced such classics as *The Amazing Colossal Man* (1957), *Tormented* (1960), *The Food of the Gods* (1976), and *Satan's Princess* (1989).

Ant farms were placed in some theater lobbies as part of a promotional campaign.

Joan Collins is best known for her role as Alexis Carrington Colby on the long-running series *Dynasty* (1981-89).

## CURSE OF THE BLACK WIDOW (1977)

Director – Dan Curtis

Writer(s) – Robert Blees

Starring – Donna Mills / Anthony Franciosa / Vic Morrow / June Allyson / Patty Duke / June Lockhart / Sid Caesar

Distributor – ABC

Released – Sept. 16, 1977

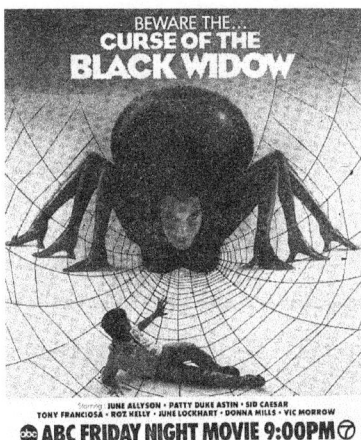

## Story:

Investigating a series of murders where the victims are wrapped in cocoons. His investiagtion leads him into a confrontation with a woman who can transform into a black widow spider.

## Cool Stuff:

Dan Curtis produced the popular TV series *Dark Shadows* (1966-71). He also directed *Trilogy of Terror* (1975) and *Burnt Offerings* (1976).

Anthony Franciosa appeared in Dario Argento's *Tenebrae* (1982).

Donna Mills has appeared in *Play Misty for Me* (1971) and *Night of Terror* (1972).

June Lockhart is best known for portaying Moareen Robinson on the series *Lost in Space* (1965-68).

Vic Morrow has appeared in numerous TV shows and films. Sadly, he was killed on the set of *Twilight Zone: The Movie* (1982).

## KINGDOM OF THE SPIDERS (1977)

*"A Living, Crawling Hell on Earth."*

Director – John" Bud" Cardos

Writer(s) – Alan Caillou / Richard Robinson / Jeffrey M. Sneller / Stephen Lodge

Starring – William Shatner / Tiffany Bolling / Woody Strode / Lieux Dressler

Distributor – Dimension Pictures

Released – Nov. 23, 1977

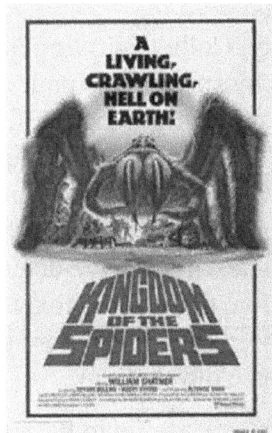

*Story:*

Rack Hansen (William Shatner) answers a call from a farmer—Walter Colby (Woody Strode). Colby's prize calf is sick, but after an examination that offers no explanation, the calf ends up dying. Rack sends some blood samples to a university for study.

Several days later, an arachnologist—Diane Ashley (Tiffany Bolling)—arrives with news. She tells Hansen that the calf died from spider venom. He doesn't believe her at first, but when Colby's dog dies, Ashley does an on-the-spot test and finds it also died of spider venom. Colby takes them to a large spider mound on his farm. Ashley says the spiders are definitely responsible, explaining that overuse of pesticides has killed off the spider's food source. While the trio is still at the farm, a bull comes rushing out of the barn, covered by spiders. Colby throws gasoline on the bull—burning it and the spiders. It seems that Ashley is correct, and the attack on the bull is just one step closer to the spiders attacking people.

The following day, Colby is driving in his truck, when is attacked by spiders that pour over him inside the cab. He attempts to fight them off, which causes him to crash—killing him. Hansen happens upon the wreck and finds Colby's dead body encased in a cocoon. Meanwhile, Ashley receives a call from her university colleagues. They have determined that the spider venom is five times more toxic than a normal spider. Then Hansen then finds more spider mounds have sprung up on Colby's farm.

The sheriff and mayor decide to have the entire farm and surrounding area saturated with pesticide—even though Ashley warns them that the pesticide is the reason for the spider's aggression to being with. She suggests using birds and rats to take care of the spiders, but hey ignore her, not wanting to disrupt the upcoming county fair. When a pilot flies up to disperse the pesticide, he is also attacked by the spiders and crashes the plane.

The spiders soon begin swarming over the town, killing and causing accidents all over town. Hansen goes to his sister-in-law's house to find her dead—and covered in spiders. But, he does manage to rescue her daughter, Linda. He, Ashley and Linda make their way to a campground—where they hide, with several others, in the lodge. But, they are soon surrounded by thousands of spiders.

In town, the assault continues. People are running everywhere, trying to escape the spiders—many die in the attempt. Even the sheriff, finally realizing that he has made a mistake, is killed after he crashes into a water tower—which falls on his vehicle, crushing him.

At the lodge, the small group begins boarding up the windows and doors. But, when the power goes out, Hansen goes into the basement and restores power. While there, a mass of tarantulas spill into the window and drop on him. He manages to make it upstairs, where he is rescued by Ashley.

He survives the night, and when he awakes, the light from outside is bright. Thinking it is all over; they peel back a board and look outside. The camera slowly pans out, revealing that the entire town has been cocooned by the spider's webbing.

This is my favorite of the "killer bug/rampaging nature" films. The acting is average, but the terror caused by so many spiders can be very frightening to the audience. There's just something about thousands of tarantulas trying to eat you that just creeps you out. I'd rather have a giant spider after me. The spider scenes were every convincing and make up for any of the film's failures. The final scene—which is a matte painting—is still pretty damn creepy. If you like—or are scared by—killer spiders, this is a must-see film.

_Cool Stuff:_

The film was nominated for best picture from the Academy of Science Fiction, Fantasy, and Horror Films (it lost to _The Little Girl Who Lives Down the Lane_). Shatner performed a spoken-word rendition of Elton John's "Rocket Man" at the ceremony—and, yes, you can find it on YouTube.

The budget was a mere $500,000.

Director, John Cardos, was also an actor, having appeared in such films as _Nightmare in Wax_ (1969), _Satan's Sadists_ (1969), and _Hell's Bloody Devils_ (1970).

William Shatner is (of course) best known as Captain Kirk on the original _Star Trek_ TV series/films. Plus numerous other projects.

Tiffany Bolling was cast, primarily, because she was not afraid of spiders. She has appeared on many TV shows, such as _Charlie's Angels_, _Night Gallery_, _The Mod Squad_ and _The New People_. Her mother, Bettie Bolling was also in the film—as Mildred, the telephone operator.

Prior to the film, Leiux Dressler appeared in many 1970's TV series, such as _Gunsmoke_, _Kolchak: The Night Stalker_, _Police Woman_, _Baretta_, and _The Rockford Files_.

Natasha Ryan, who plays the daughter, Linda, is probably best known for her short, but occurring role on the soap opera, _Days of Our Lives_, and on the series, _Ladies' Man_.

Many of the actors/extras suffered bouts of itching/redness—due to the spider's bristles. It is a method that tarantulas use to fend off predators. They shake loose some of their tiny hairs, which irritate skin and can complicate breathing. Unless you are allergic to it, tarantula venom is no more harmful than a bee sting.

Most of the music was culled from episodes of *The Twilight Zone*.

A sequel was scheduled, with Shatner returning and directing, but (thankfully?) was never produced.

5,000 tarantulas were used in the film. Handlers were paid $10 per spider—10% of the film's entire budget.

Bo Svenson (of *Walking Tall* fame) turned down the role.

Sadly, many spiders were, unintentionally, killed during filming (The film would have to use different methods today to avoid such cruelty).

## IT HAPPENED AT LAKEWOOD MANOR (aka ANTS) (1977)

*"The Picnic Is Ruined"*

Director – Robert Scheerer

Writer(s) – Guerdon Trueblood

Starring – Robert Fox worth / Suzanne Somers /
Bernie Casey

Distributor – ABC

Released – Dec. 2, 1977

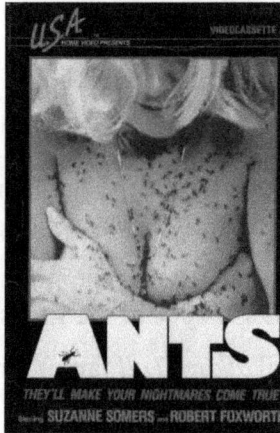

## Story:

A wealthy real estate tycoon, and his mistress, seek to
purchase the floundering Lakewood Hotel and turn it
into a casino. But, their plans go unfinished, as an
army of ants begin attacking everyone in the hotel.

## Cool Stuff:

Robert Scheerer directed episodes for many popular
TV series—such as *Fame* (1982-84), *The Love Boat*
(1981-86), *Dynasty* (1983-87), and *Star Trek: The
Next Generation* (1989-93).

The film starred many TV series of the era—Robert
Foxworth (*Men at Law*), Lynda Day George (*Mission*

*Impossible*), Bernie Casey (*Harris and Company*), and Gerald Gordon (*The Doctors*).

Suzanne Somers went on to fame, following the film's release, as Chrissy on *Three's Company* (1977-81).

## TARANTULAS: THE DEADLY CARGO (1977)

*"Terror & death sweep through a defenseless town!"*

Director – Stuart Hagmann

Writer(s) – John Groves / Guerdon Trueblood

Starring – Claude Akins / Deborah Winters

Distributor – CBS

Released – Dec. 28, 1977

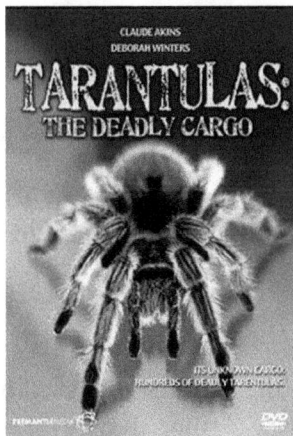

*Story:*

On its way from South America, a plane carrying coffee bean crashes into a small California town. What no one knows, is that a group of deadly tarantulas were aboard. After the crash, the spiders begin terrorizing workers at an orange factory—and set their sights on the town.

*Cool Stuff:*

Claude Akins had appeared in over 300 films and TV shows in his 40+ year career.

Tom Atkins also appeared in *The Fog* (1980), *Escape from New York* (1981), *Halloween III: Season of the Witch* (1982), and *Night of the Creeps* (1986).

Guerdon Trueblood wrote the story for *Jaws 3-D* (1983).

The film was nominated for 2 Emmys—Sound Editing for a Special and Sound Mixing.

## THE SWARM (1978)

*"It's more than a speculation—it's a prediction!"*

Director – Irwin Allen

Writer(s) – Stirling Silliphant / based on the novel by Arthur Herzog

Starring – Michael Caine / Richard Chamberlain /
Katherine Ross / Lee Grant

Distributor – Warner Bros.

Released – July 14, 1978

## Story:

Killer bees attack the city of Houston, Texas—and a bunch of popular actors fight them.

## Cool Stuff:

Irwin Allen produced several very popular TV series in the 1960s—*The Time Tunnel* (1966-67), *Lost in Space* (1965-68), *Voyage to the Bottom of the Sea* (1964-68), and *Land of the Giants* (1968-70). He also produced several "disaster" films—*The Poseidon Adventure* (1972), *The Towering Inferno* (1974), and *Flood* (1976).

Arthur Herzog also wrote *Orca* (1977)—which was made into a film by Dino De Laurentiis.

Of the 22 million bees used in the film, 800,000 had their stingers removed to avoid any painful incidents with actors.

## THE BEES (1978)

*"They prey on Human Flesh!"*

Director – Alfredo Zacarias

Writer(s) – Alfredo Zacarias / Jack Hill

Starring – John Saxon / Angel Tompkins / John Carradine

Distributor – New World Pictures

Released – Nov. 1978

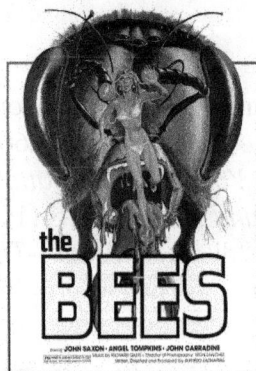

*Story:*

When South American killer bees are smuggled into the U.S.—they begin terrorizing the populace.

*Cool Stuff:*

As with *The Swarm*, the bees had their stingers removed—so they wouldn't harm the crew.

The movie was filmed in Mexico, and each scene was filmed twice so the dubbing would be a perfect match.

Warner Brothers reportedly paid New World Pictures to delay the film's release, so it wouldn't have to compete with *The Swarm*.

## THE FLY (1986)

*"Be Afraid. Be Very Afraid."*

Director - David Cronenberg

Writer(s) – Charles Edward Pogue / David Cronenberg / based on the story by George Langelaan

Starring – Jeff Goldblum / Geena Davis / John Getz

Distributor – 20th Century Fox

Released – Aug. 15, 1986

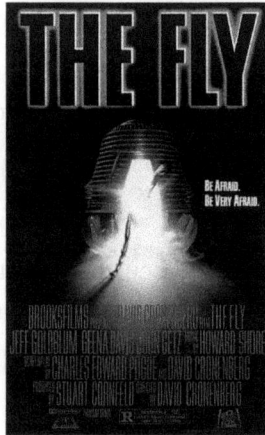

### Story:

Scientist, Seth Brundle (Jeff Goldblum), convinces journalist Veronica Quaife (Geena Davis) to come see a project, which he claims will change the world. When they arrive at his warehouse, Quaife finds that Brundle has created "telepods", which allows him to transport an object from one pod to another. Intrigued, Quaife agrees to document Brundle's experiments. They also develop a romantic relationship.

One experiment involves transporting a baboon—which ends badly, as the baboon is killed. A second attempt is successful, and Brundle is ecstatic. But, when Quaife suddenly leaves, Brundle suspects she is trying to rekindle her relationship with her magazine editor, Stathis Borans (John Getz).

Angry, and drunk, Brundle climbs into the telepod and transports himself—successfully. But, unknown to Brundle, a fly was in the telepod with him. He begins to exhibit extraordinary abilities, and when

Quaife returns, Brundle wants her to teleport as well. Though she wants to be with him, she is afraid to attempt the teleportation. Brundle kicks her out, telling her she is weak. While Quaife is gone, Brundle picks up a prostitute. Quaife catches the two together and sees that Brundle is looking sick. She convinces the prostitute to leave, then Brundle kicks Quaife out as well.

Brundle continues to change—his fingernails and teeth are falling out, his skin looks cancerous, and his appetite increases, though he must vomit on his food, to dissolve it, before consumption. Brundle realizes that the computer, finding two separate entities in the pod, did not know how to keep them separate—and decided to fuse Brundle with the fly, which created Brundle-Fly.

Quaife returns to inform Brundle that she is pregnant with his child. After a dream—where she gives birth to a maggot—she is confused and afraid. Brundle tries to convince her that the only way to help him, is to have her in the telepod with him—mixing their DNA. Borans, who followed Quaife to the warehouse, confronts Brundle with a shotgun, but Brundle overpowers him—then vomits on Borans' arm and ankle, dissolving them.

Brundle then tries to force Quaife into the pods, she fights against him and accidently rips off his jaw. But, the Bundlefly's strength is too much, and he/it pushes her into one pod. He steps into the second pod, but Borans manages to grab the shotgun—with his remaining hand—and shoots the cables of the telepod that Quaife is in. She escapes, but Brundle is teleported to the third pod—but, a malfunction fuses his body with some of the metal of the pod.

Quaife grabs the shotgun, but when she fails to pull the trigger, Brundle reaches up and pulls the shotgun to his head, begging her to put him out of his misery. She does.

### *Cool Stuff:*

Director, David Cronenberg, has directed numerous classic Horror films—such as *Scanners* (1981), *Videodrome* (1983), and *eXistenZ* (1999).

Of course, we know Jeff Goldblum from such classics as – *Invasion of the Body Snatchers* (1978), *Jurassic Park* (1993), and *Independence Day* (1996).

Geena Davis can be found in the classic *Beetlejuice* (1988), as well as the brilliant *A League of Their Own* (1992).

Comedy legend, Mel Brooks, produced the film—but didn't want anyone to know it because he was afraid people wouldn't take the film seriously.

Chris Walas, who did the creature effects, won an Oscar for his work. And he went on to direct the sequel.

Michael Keaton turned down the role of Seth Brundle.

Jeff Goldblum often had to wear 5lbs of prosthetics, some of which took 5 hours to apply.

David Cronenberg has a cameo in the film—he is the doctor who delivers the maggot baby in Quaife's dream sequence.

## BLUE MONKEY (1987)

*"They Breed. They Hatch. They Kill."*

Director – William Fruet

Writer(s) – George Goldsmith / Chris Koseluk

Starring – Steve Railsback / Ivan R. Roth / Gwynyth Walsh

Distributor – International Spectrafilm

Released – Sept. 25, 1987

*Story:*

After being bitten by an insect, a man is hospitalized. Soon after, an alien parasite breaks out of his skin and—after growing larger—begins terrorizing the hospital residents.

*Cool Stuff:*

The original title, *The Green Monkey*, was changed because it was believed, by some, that AIDS was transmitted by green monkeys.

Director William Fruet went on to direct numerous TV episodes of several popular Sci-Fi shows—such as *War of the Worlds* (1988-90), *Goosebumps* (1995-98), and *Poltergeist: The Legacy* (1997-99).

George Goldsmith also wrote the screenplay for Stephen King's *Children of the Corn* (1984).

## EVIL SPAWN (1987)

*"Tonight, She Will Love Again and Kill Again"*

Director – Kenneth J. Hall / Ted Newsom / Fred Olen Ray

Writer – Kenneth J. Hall / Ted Newsom

Starring – Bobbie Bresee / Drew Godderis / Dawn Wildsmith

Distributor – AIP

Released – Dec. 31, 1987

_Story:_

After being bitten by an insect, a man is hospitalized. Soon after, an alien parasite breaks out of his skin and—after growing larger—begins terrorizing the hospital residents.

_Cool Stuff:_

The film had a bumpy road to completion. It went through multiple directors and was re-edited by Fred Olen Ray and re-released as _The Alien Within_.

The gorgeous Bobbie Bresee also starred/appeared in _Mausoleum_ (1983), _Ghoulies_ (1984), and _Surf Nazis Must Die_ (1987).

Fred Olen Ray has produced/written/directed/or acted in over 200 films. Among them such classics as— _Sleazemania!_ (1985), _Hollywood Chainsaw Hookers_

(1988), *Beverly Hills Vamp* (1989), *Evil Toons* (1992), *Attack of the 60 Foot Centerfold* (1995), the TV series *Dante's Cove* (2006-07) and *The Lair* (2007-09).

## SLUGS (1988)

*"No-one is Safe!"*

Director - Juan Piquer Simon

Writer(s) – Juan Piquer Simon / Ron Gantman / based on the novel by Shaun Hutson

Starring – Michael Garfield / Kim Terry

Distributor – New World Pictures

Released – Feb. 1988

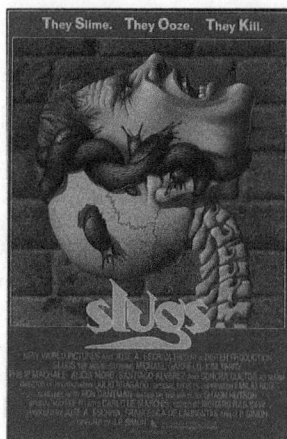

*Story:*

A small town has been used for toxic waste dumping. A radiation from the waste creates an army of killer slugs that begin killing the local populace.

*Cool Stuff:*

The film is based on the novel, *Slugs* by Shaun Hutson.

Michael Garfield appeared as Rogue in *The Warriors* (1979).

It was originally banned in Queensland, Australia—until the 1990s.

## THE NEST (1988)

*"The Terror Has Hatched"*

Director – Terence H. Winkless

Writer(s) – Robert King

Starring – Robert Lansing / Lisa Langlois / Terri Treas

Distributor – MGM

Released – May 13, 1988

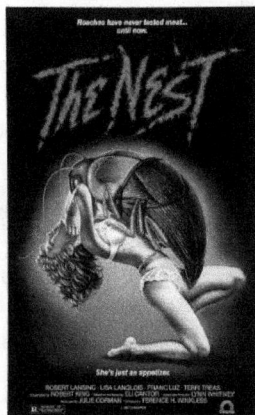

*Story:*

When pets and people start vanishing, a Sheriff soon finds that his island town is being terrorized by mutant cockroaches—which are being bred by a corrupt organization.

*Cool Stuff:*

The film was produced by Julie Corman (wife to Roger Corman). She produced other genre classics, like *Saturday the 14th* (1981), *Chopping Mall* (1986), and *Brain Dead* (1990).

The roaches used in the film were actually found on the street—and made stars. They also stuck around the studio for several years following filming.

The film was completed in 25 days.

This was the directorial debut of Terence H. Winkless—who went on to direct numerous films and

TV shows. He directed 38 episodes of *Mighty Morphin Power Rangers* (1993-95).

The film is based on the novel, *The Nest* by Gregory A. Douglas (aka Eli Cantor).

### THE FLY II (1989)

*"A New Generation of Terror!"*

Director – Chris Walas

Writer(s) – Mick Garris / Frank Darabont

Starring – Eric Stoltz / Daphne Zuniga / Lee Richardson / John Getz

Distributor – 20$^{th}$ Century Fox

Released – Feb. 10, 1989

## Story:

A direct sequel to the 1986 film—*The Fly*—finds the son of Seth Brundle (Martin) being raised under the watchful eye of a corrupt corporation. Martin seeks to find a way to cure the dormant mutated genes that threaten to come to life.

## Cool Stuff:

Director Chris Walas created the incredible effects for David Cronenberg's *The Fly* (1986), as well as *Scanners* (1981), *Raiders of the Lost Ark* (1981), and *Gremlins* (1984).

The Telepods had to be reconstructed, as the original props (from the previous film) were destroyed.

Geena Davis turned down reappearing in the film, as her character dies early in the film. It is also believed that she had been so upset from the previous films "maggot baby" sequence.

Eric Stoltz has appeared in numerous films, such as *The Prophecy* (1995), *The Butterfly Effect* (2004), and the TV mini-series, *The Triangle* (2005).

Daphne Zuniga voiced Princess Vespa in *Spaceballs: The Animated Series* (2008-09)

John Getz is the only actor—from the previous film—to return.

The film was originally rated X, but Walas convinced the MPAA to give it an R.

We almost had Keanu Reeves, but he turned down the role of Martin Brundle.

## ARACHNOPHOBIA (1990)

*"Eight Legs, Two Fangs and An Attitude."*

Director – Frank Marshall

Writers – Don Jakoby / Wesley Strick (based on a story by Don Jakoby / Al Williams)

Starring – Jeff Daniels / Harley Jane Kozak / John Goodman / Julian Sands

Distributor – Buena Vista Pictures

Released – July 18, 1990

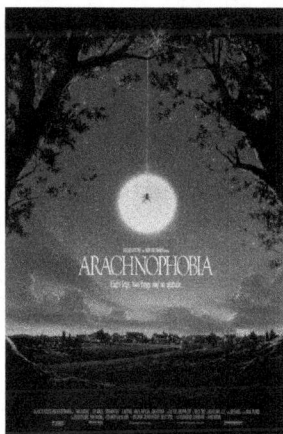

<u>*Story:*</u>

The film begins in the Amazon rainforest, where entomologist James Atherton (Julian Sands), leads a team, all hoping to discover new species of insects or arachnids. Traveling with them is a photographer Jerry Manley (Mark L. Taylor). After discovering a new spider, they return to camp. Unknown to anyone, another spider has climbed into Manley's backpack. While the researchers are studying their finds, Manley attempts to take a nap, but the spider bites him— killing him. Thinking he died of a fever, the team boxes up his body and sends it home—but it has another passenger, the deadly spider.

The body arrives home to a small California town named, Canaima. At the same time, a new doctor, Ross Jennings (Jeff Daniels), and his family are just moving in. The spider escapes the makeshift coffin and is picked up by a crow. Biting the crow, it drops onto the Jennings family's new farm. Ross, thinking he is to be the new town doctor, finds out the town's current doctor, Sam Metcalf (Henry Jones) does not want to retire—forcing Ross to wonder what they will do now. He finds one ally, Margaret Hollins (Mary Carver), who becomes Ross's first patient.

Meanwhile, the Amazonian spider mates with a domestic spider, who then builds a nest in the Jennings' barn. Margaret throws a party for the Jennings family, hoping the town will accept him. But, after Margaret dies of an apparent heart attack and a high school football player (both of whom were seen by Jennings), the town starts calling him Dr. Death, not knowing they died of spider bites.

We then meet exterminator Delbert McClintock (John Goodman), who begins looking for spiders after the high school coach's daughter encounters one in the shower. Finding no evidence of a spider, Delbert leaves the house and encounters one of the spiders on the outside walkway. He sprays it, but the poison has not effect. He then steps on it.

Then, after Dr. Metcalf dies, Ross does an autopsy on the bodies, which reveals that both may have died from spider bites. Ross contacts Atherton—who remembers that Manley was part of his team—and sends an assistant, Chris Collins (Brian McNamara) to Canaima. Ross, Chris, the coroner, and the sheriff begin a search for the spiders, where they finally find a live specimen. Chris calls Atherton and tells him he needs to get here now.

Soon, the ever-growing group determines that the offspring of the Amazonian spider (now dubbed the General) and a house spider, has produced an army—which, it seems, will likely decimate the local area as they spread, killing everything is their path. They need to find the nest and kill the queen. Atherton is killed while investigating the barn. Ross, Collins and Delbert realize that the spiders are at the Jennings' home. They arrive, find that Atherton is dead, and then go the house. Jennings' family is watching TV, but the house is soon overrun with spiders. Everyone tries to escape and end up climbing outside.

Ross gets trapped inside, and tries to make his way downstairs, but falls from the second floor and crashes through the first floor—landing in the basement. It is there that he discovers the spider's egg sack. Ross manages to kill the queen, but when he attempts to destroy the egg sack, the General startles him and Ross falls to the floor, trapping himself under a full wine rack. He manages to fight off the spider (overcoming his own arachnophobia) and sends it flying across the room where it catches on fire. Then Ross fires a nail gun, sending the General into the egg sack—where spider and egg sack pops and burns, killing the offspring.

The Jennings family moves back to San Francisco.

A very effective entry made with seeming care and enthusiasm. The spiders—utilizing the brilliant work of spider wranglers, Steve Kutcher, and Jules Sylvester—were wonderfully entertaining, and even a little creepy. Many filmgoers found the film funny while others cringed in fear when the spiders appeared on the screen. Though laced with much humor, you won't be disappointed if you want a film that makes your skin crawl—or, at least, makes you feel like something is crawling on you.

## *Cool Stuff:*

Director Frank Marshall is best known for his production work (many in collaboration with his wife, Kathleen Kennedy, and director Stephen Spielberg) of some of the best movies of all-time. From, *The Warriors* (1979), *Raiders of the Lost Ark* (1981), *Poltergeist* (1982), *Gremlins* (1984), *Back to the Future* (1985), and *Who Framed Roger Rabbit?* (1988).

Jeff Daniels has been many diverse films—such as *Dumb & Dumber* (1994), *Speed* (1994), and *Looper* (2012)—as well as such TV shows as the recent, *The Newsroom* (2012-2014).

Harely Jane Kozak has been in numerous films (like *Parenthood*—1989) but has primarily been associated with TV, having been in shows like—*Knightwatch* (1988-89), *Harts of the West* (1993-94), and *You Wish* (1997-98).

John Goodman—he of *Roseanne* (1988-1997) fame—has been all over the place, gracing us with his performances in *King Ralph* (1991) and *The Flintstones* (1994), to *The Big Lebowski* (1998) and *Coyote Ugly* (2000), to *O Brother Where Art Thou?* (2000) and *Monsters Inc.* (2001).

Julian Sands is probably best known to genre fans for such films as *Gothic* (1986), *Warlock* (1988), and most recently, as Gerald Crane on the TV series, *Gotham* (2014-).

Dan Jakoby also wrote the screenplays for *Lifeforce* (1985), *Invaders from Mars* (1986), and *Vampires* (1998).

The sound of the spider, that is crushed under John Goodman's foot, is actually potato chips being crushed.

The primary spiders used in the film are a harmless species known as (Avondale spiders), from New Zealand. The larger spider used in the film's opening is that of the bird-eating tarantula.

The spiders in the film were handled by entomologist Steven Kutcher—who "bug wrangled" in such films as *Prince of Darkness* (1987), *Leprechaun 2* (1994), and *Mimic* (1997).

The film was the first one released under the Hollywood Pictures label.

The large animatronic spider (aka the General), used for the film's final act, was created by future Mythbuster, Jamie Hyneman.

The film won the Saturn Award (from the Academy of Science Fiction, Fantasy and Horror Films) for Best Horror Film and Best Actor (Jeff Daniels).

The film was scored by Trevor Jones, who also scored *Excalibur* (1981), *Time Bandits* (1981), *The Dark Crystal* (1982), *Labyrinth* (1986), and *Angel Heart* (1987).

A video game of the film was released in 1991—for the Commodore 64, Amiga and DOS.

It was a successful film—grossing nearly $54 million (on $8 million budget). Even more impressive, it made over $30 million in video rentals.

## SKEETER (1993)

*"An Environmental Disaster With A Name."*

Director - Clark Brandon

Writer(s) – Clark Brandon / Lanny Horn / Joseph Luis Rubin

Starring – Jim Youngs / Tracy Griffith

Distributor – August Entertainment

Released – Apr. 6, 1994 (USA)

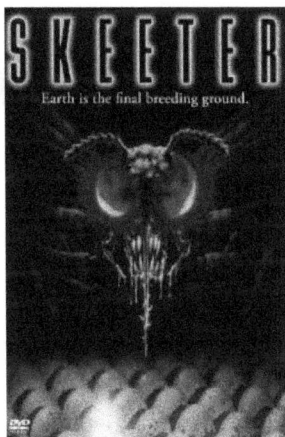

*Story:*

A small-town sheriff discovers that toxic waste has been dumped into the mines—which has resulted in the mutation of mosquitoes, who have grown to terrifying proportions and begins attacking residents.

*Cool Stuff:*

Star Tracy Griffith (half-sister to Melanie Griffith) has starred in the genre favorites *Sleepaway Camp III: Teenage Wasteland* (1989) and *The First Power* (1990).

Charles Napier-who appeared in over 200 films/TV shows before his death in 2011, also starred in such cult classics as *Beyond the Valley of the Dolls* (1970), *Supervixens* (1975), *The Blues Brothers* (1980), and the TV series *The Incredible Hulk* (1979-82).

## TICKS (1994)

*"They Breed. They Hatch. They Kill."*

Director – Tony Randel

Writer(s) – Brent V. Friedman

Starring – Peter Scolari / Seth Green / Rosalind Allen / Ami Dolenz / Alfonso Riberio

Distributor – Republic Pictures

Released – May 25, 1994

### *Story:*

A couple takes a group of problem teens on a "getting in touch with nature" trip. While there, they encounter some pot growers—who have been using steroids to increase their yield. Unbeknownst to the growers, ticks have gotten into the pot and have grown to cat-sized monsters.

The teens—and their counselors—are soon in a battle for their lives against the killer ticks.

*Cool Stuff:*

Director Tony Randel also directed *Hellbound: Hellraiser II* (1988) and 23 episodes of the TV series *Beyond Belief: Fact or Fiction* (1998-2002).

Seth Green is a genre icon, having appeared in or creating numerous shows. He is probably best known for his role as Oz on *Buffy, The Vampire Slayer* (1997-2002), and creator of the Adult Swim animated series *Robot Chicken* (2005-2016), as well as being a voice actor for many animated shows.

Ami Dolenz is the daughter of Micky Dolenz (of The Monkees) and has appeared in numerous films/TV shows—such as *Witchboard 2* (1993), *Pumpkinhead II: Blood Wings* (1993), and *House Rules for Bad Girls* (2009).

Alphonso Ribeiro appeared as Carlton on the long-running TV series, *The Fresh Prince of Bel-Air* (1990-96).

Visual Effects Supervisor Doug Beswick also created various visual effects for *Beetlejuice* (1988), *Blade* (1998), *Frailty* (2001), and *Pulse* (2006).

The film was made for about $2 million and completed in just five weeks.

## DEADLY INVASION: THE KILLER BEE NIGHTMARE (1995)

*"Your worst fears can come true!"*

Director – Rockne S. O'Bannon

Writer(s) – William Bast / Paul Huson

Starring – Robert Hayes / Nancy Stafford / Ryan Phillipe / Dennis Christopher

Distributor – Fox

Released – Feb. 28, 1995

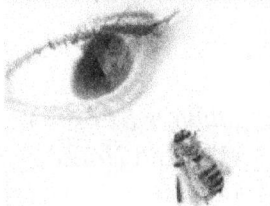

## Story:

After moving from Boston to a small California town, a family battles for survival after their farm house is attacked by a swarm of killer bees.

_Cool Stuff:_

Rockne S. O'Bannon has written, directed and produced numerous genre projects—such as _The Twilight Zone_ (1985-87), _Alien Nation_ (1988-90), _SeaQuest 2023_ (1993-95), _Farscape_ (1999-2003), and _Defiance_ (2013-14).

William Bast wrote the screenplay for Ray Harryhausen's _The Valley of Gwangi_ (1969).

Ryan Phillippe started out as a daytime TV star, then went on to star in _I Know What You Did Last Summer_ (1997), _Cruel Intentions_ (1998), and others.

Gina Phlips appeared in _Jeepers Creepers_ (2001).

Dennis Christopher starred in _Fade to Black_ (1980).

## MOSQUITO (aka BLOOD FEVER) (1995)

_"Blood Never Tasted Better."_

Director – Gary Jones

Writer(s) – Tom Chaney / Steve Hodge / Gary Jones

Starring – Gunnar Hansen / Steve Dixon / Ron Asheton

Distributor – Helmdale

Released – May 20, 1995

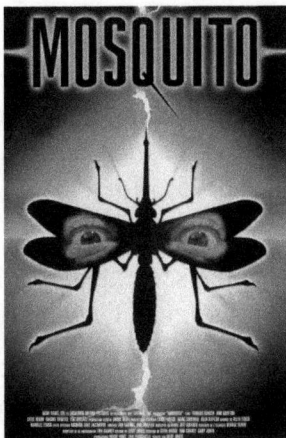

*Story:*

An alien ship dumps their trash in a U.S. Park—creating giant mosquitoes that go on a killing spree. No human is safe.

*Cool Stuff:*

Gunnar Hansen is best known for his portrayal of Leatherface in *The Texas Chainsaw Massacre* (1974).

Ron Asheton is the lead guitarist of The Stooges.

While filming a nude scene—inside a tent—Margaret Gomoll was injured when a camera fell on her head.

The film was made with a meager budget of $200,000.

## JOE'S APARTMENT (1996)

*"Sex, Bugs, Rock N' Roll"*

Director/Writer – John Payson

Starring – Jerry O'Connell / Megan Ward

Distributor – Warner Bros.

Released – July 26, 1996

### Story:

A jobless college graduate takes a job running a rent-controlled apartment building and finds that, in addition to humans, it is occupied by talking/dancing/singing cockroaches—who quickly become his best friends.

### Cool Stuff:

Jerry O'Connell also starred in the TV series *Sliders* (1995-2000) and as Vern, in the Stephen King film, *Stand By Me* (1986).

Megan Ward has starred in the TV series *Dark Skies* (1996-97).

Robert Vaughn is best known as Napoleon Solo on the TV series, *The Man from U.N.C.L.E.* (1964-68).

The cockroaches were created with a combination of live roaches, stop-motion animation, puppets, and CGI.

This was the first feature film produced by MTV.

Bill West voiced the cockroach, Ralph, and has done voice work for numerous animated shows—such as *Pinky and the Brain* (1997-98), *Voltron: The Third Dimension* (1998-2000), *Men in Black: The Series* (1997-2001), *CatDog* (1998-2005), and *Futurama* (1999-2013)-where he voices several characters.

Reginald Hudlin has produced, written and directed many programs, like *The House Party* films (1990-91) and *The Boondocks* (2005-08). He has also written comic books, the most well-known being Black Panther.

Comedian Dave Chappelle provides some of the voice work for the roaches.

## MIMIC (1997)

*"For thousands of years, man had been evolution's greatest creation...until now."*

Director – Guillermo del Toro

Writer(s) – Matthew Robbins / Guillermo del Toro / based on the story by Donald A. Wollheim

Starring – Mira Sorvino / Jeremy Northram / Josh Brolin / Charles S. Dutton / Giancarlo Giannini / F. Murray Abraham

Distributor – Miramax Films

Released – Aug. 22, 1997

*Story:*

An entomologist, Susan (Mira Sorvino), creates an insect, whose enzymes kill off diseased roaches. But, when the new insect gets in the general population—a deadly breed is produced. Several years later, this new breed soon evolves into a giant, human-like creature, which feeds on people.

Susan puts together a small group and descends into the tunnels beneath the city, in an attempt, to find and destroy creatures.

## Cool Stuff:

Director Guillermo del Toro is an icon in the Horror/Fantasy/Sci-Fi genre, having created such classics as—*Cronos* (1993), *The Devils Backbone* (2001), *Hellboy* (2004), *Pan's Labyrinth* (2006), and *Pacific Rim* (2013). He was unhappy with the film because he didn't get a final cut. He did release a director's cut in 2011. He also butted heads with producers Harvey and Bob Weinstein (and never worked for them again).

Mira Sorvino has appeared in numerous films/TV series, such as—including *The Replacement Killers* (1998), *The Final Cut* (2004), and the recent *Falling Skies* (2014-15),

Charles S. Dutton played Dillon in *Alien 3* (1992) and as Roc Emerson in the long-running series, *Roc* (1991-94).

Jeremy Northram has appeared in *The Net* (1995), *The Invasion* (2007), and as Sir Thomas More in the TV series, *The Tudors* (2007-08).

This was the film debut of Norman Reedus, best known for his portrayal of Daryl Dixon on *The Walking Dead* (2010-). He also appeared in Blade II (2002) and as Paige's boyfriend, Nate, on the TV series Charmed (1998-2006).

F. Murray Abraham won an Academy Award for his role as Antonio Salieri in *Amadeus* (1984).

Josh Brolin first appeared in the classic, *The Goonies* (1985), but has been in many films we love—such as *Hollow Man* (2000), *Planet Terror* (2007), *Men in Black 3* (2012), but he's probably best known as Thanos in *Avengers: Infinity War* (2018) and Cable in *Deadpool 2* (2018).

Giancarlo Gianni has appeared in over 160 films, such as *Black Belly of the Tarantula* (1971), the *Dune* TV Mini-Series (2000), *Darkness* (2002), and as Rene Mathis in the Bond films *Casino Royale* (2006) and *Quantum of Solace* (2008).

## STARSHIP TROOPERS (1997)

*"A New Kind of Enemy. A New Kind of War."*

Director – Paul Verhoeven

Writer(s) – Edward Neimeier / based on the novel by Robert A. Heinlein (loosely)

Starring – Casper Van Dien / Denise Richards / Dina Meyer / Patrick Muldoon / Jake Busey /Neil Patrick Harris / Michael Ironside

Distributor – Tri-Star Pictures

Released – Nov. 7, 1997

_Story:_

It's the 23<sup>rd</sup> century, and humans begun colonizing planets in the far reaches of space. One such planet is Klendathu—which is populated with insect/arachnid creatures who have not taken kindly to the Earthlings that have come to their planet. As such, a war breaks out between the two planets.

On Earth, a group of high school graduates are planning their futures. Johnny Rico (Casper Van Dien), his girlfriend Carmen Ibanez (Denise Richards), Dizzy Flores (Dina Meyer), who has a crush on Rico, and Carl Jenkins (Neil Patrick Harris) are among the graduates. They all enlist with the Federal Service—which guarantees citizenship (a position of privilege above normal citizens). While Carmen qualifies for pilot, Rico is forced to join the Mobile Infantry—which Dizzy will be part of.

During training, Carmen sends Rico a video message where she tells him she plans to become a captain—which will leave no time for them as a couple. Rico

become a squad leader, but when a trainee is killed, Rico is punished and decides to quit. But, before he can leave, news comes that his home of Buenos Aires has been destroyed by an asteroid sent by the "bugs" from Klendathu. The two planets are now, officially at war.

Rico, Dizzy and Ace (Jake Busey) join the fight, and when Rico kills one of the giant Tanker Bugs, he is promoted and his squad becomes known as Rico's Roughnecks. During the numerous battles, Rico and Dizzy finally hook up, but she is killed by one of the Arachnids. The ship that rescues them is piloted by Carmen—and her new boyfriend, Zander (Patrick Muldoon).

A final battle causes Carmen's ship to crash into Klendathu. Rico's Roughnecks ignore orders and goes to finds her. Zander is killed, but the Roughnecks manage to rescue Carmen and when they emerge from the caves, they find that one of the Brain Bugs that has been captured and that the war has changed—as they now know that the Arachnids know fear.

But, the war continues—with Carmen commanding her own ship and Rico as a commanding officer.

### Cool Stuff:

The film is based on the 1959 novel by Robert A. Heinlein

Paul Verhoevon also directed *Robocop* (1987), *Total Recall* (1990), and *Hollow Man* (2000)—as well as the controversial *Showgirls* (1995).

Casper Van Dien has starred in over 100 films, including such genre films as *Sleepy Hollow* (1999), *Dracula 3000* (2005), and a slew of TV movies, like *Python* (2000), *The Vector File* (2002), *Skeleton Man* (2004), and *The Curse of King Tut's Tomb* (2006).

Dina Meyer is a genre icon, having appeared in *Johnny Mneumonic* (1995), *Bats* (1999), *Saw I-IV* (2004-07), *Riddles of the Sphinx* (2008), *Pirahna 3D* (2010), and as Oracle/Batgirl on the TV series *Birds of Prey* (2002-03).

Michael Ironside has appeared in over 250 films, including *Scanners* (1981), *Prom Night II* (1987), *Total Recall* (1990), *Children of the Corn: Revelation* (2001), and *Lake Placid 3* (2010). His voice work can be found in such TV series as *Superman: The Animated Series* (1997-2000), *Justice League* (2003), and *Transformers Prime* (2013).

Jake Busey actually learned to play the violin for the movie.

Though there were some robotic models, the majority of the alien arachnids were CGI.

The movie used 17 gallons of fake blood for its many graphic scenes.

In Heinlein's novel, Rico (Casper Van Dien) was Filipino.

The high school is actually a Kaiser Permanente hospital.

Casper Van Dien broke a rib, and Jake Busey suffered heat stroke during filming.

**MARABUNTA (aka LEGION OF FIRE: KILLER ANTS (1998)**

Director – Jim Charleston / George Manasse

Writer(s) – Linda Palmer / Wink Roberts

Starring – Mitch Pileggi / Eric Lutes / Julia Campbell

Distributor – Fox

Released – June 24, 1998

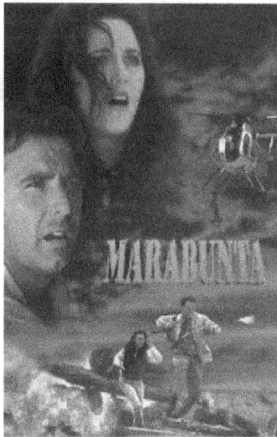

*Story:*

An earthquake unleashes a hive of killer ants onto a small Alaskan town.

*Cool Stuff:*

Eric Lutes also starred in *Legend of the Mummy* (1998).

Julia Campbell portrayed Ellen Rimbauer in the Stephen King mini-series, *Rose Red* (2002).

Mitch Pileggi is best known for portraying Walter Skinner on the TV series, *The X-Files* (1994-2018), as well as starring in *Shocker* (1989), *Stargate: Atlantis* (2005-09), and voicing Commissioner James Gordon in the animated series, *The Batman* (2005-07).

Linda Palmer (as Melinda Palmer) wrote *The Garbage Pail Kids Movie* (1987).

Wink Roberts was a stuntman on all 6 *Police Academy* films (1984-89).

**BUG BUSTER (1998)**

*"There's Something Creepy In The Neighborhood."*

Director – Lorenzo Doumani

Writer(s) – Malick Khoury

Starring – Randy Quaid / Katherine Heigl / Brenda Epperson / James Doohan / George Takei

Distributor – Prism Leisure

Released – Dec. 31, 1998

*Story:*

Killer cockroaches vs. Randy Quaid.

*Cool Stuff:*

Lorenzo Doumani also directed Storybook (1996) and Monster Night (2006).

The eccentric Randy Quaid has been in numerous films—such as *National Lampoon's Vacation* (1983), *Independence Day* (1996), *Not Another Teen Movie* (2001), *and Category 6: Day of Destruction* (2004).

Katherine Heigl starred in the TV series *Roswell* (1999-2002) before becoming a romantic comedy film star.

James Doohan played Scotty in the original TV series (and subsequent films) of *Star Trek.*

**THEY NEST (2000) - aka CREEPY CRAWLERS**

*"It's Feeding Time."*

Directors – Ellory Elkayem

Writer(s) – John Claflin / Daniel Zelman

Starring – Thomas Calabro / Kristen Dalton / Dean Stockwell

Distributor – Kushner Locke Company

Released – July 25, 2000

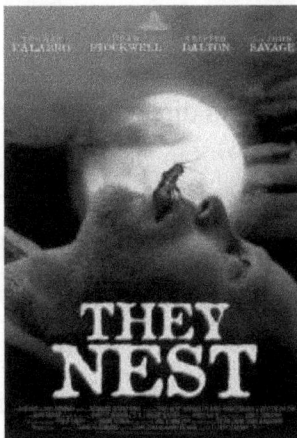

*Story:*

Alcohol and marital issues cause Dr. Ben Cahill (Thomas Calabro) to screw up in the emergency room. Hoping to get a handle on his life, Cahill goes to a house on Orr Island. He meets a local, Sheriff

Hobbs (Dean Stockwell), who asks Cahill to help him identify animal and human corpses that have strange injuries.

Cahill also meets Nell Bartle (Kristen Dalton), who seems to be the only islander who isn't treating him like an outsider. They soon find out that an army of cockroaches has invaded the island. These roaches attack and nest inside their prey. The island is soon overrun with the creatures, and our ragtag group of survivors must fight for their lives and escape the island—before they become home for the hungry roaches.

### Cool Stuff:

Ellory Elkayem also directed *Eight-Legged Freaks* (2002) and *two Return of the Living Dead* films-- *Necropolis* and *Rave to the Grave* (2005)

Dean Stockwell has been in over 200 films/TV shows--including such genre classics as *Quantum Leap* (19898-1993), *Dune* (1984), *The Shadow Men* (1997), and *Battlestar Galactica* (2006-09).

Kristen Dalton is probably best known for her portrayal as Dana Bright on the TV series *The Dead Zone (*2002-06).

Thomas Calabro is likely best known for his role as Dr. Michael Mancini on the TV series, *Melrose Place* (1992-99).

John Savage has been in over 200 films in his career. You can find him in *The Deer Hunter* (1978), *Hair* (1979), and *The Onion Field* (1979).

Terry Sonderhoff has done special effects work in such films as—*Timecop* (1994*), Bordello of Blood* (1996), *Final Destination* (2000), and *Trick r' Treat* (2007).

## ISLAND OF THE DEAD (2000)

*"Never disturb the dead."*

Director – Tim Southam

Writer(s) – Peter Koper / Tim Southam

Starring – Malcolm McDowell / Taliso Soto / Mos Def / Bruce Ramsay

Distributor – Cornerstone Films

Released – July 2000

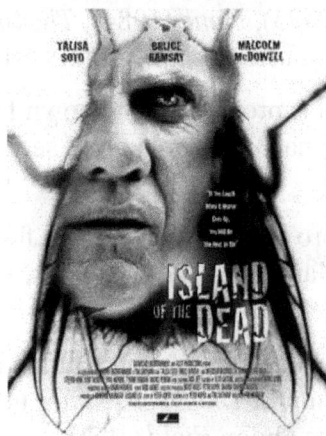

## Story:

Hart Island has a secret—the bodies of unknown people are buried there. When a greedy multi-millionaire, Mr. King (Malcolm McDowell) decides to try and turn the island into a resort, he and a small group of people soon realize that years of decaying dead has produced an army of deadly flies—and the stranded group are their meals.

## Cool Stuff:

Malcolm McDowell has been in many genre films, such as *A Clockwork Orange* (1971) & *Time After Time* (1979).

Talisa Soto played Princess Kitana in the Mortal Combat films.

Mealworms were used for the fly larvae, instead of the actual fly larvae we know as maggots.

## SPIDERS (2000)

*"Something Very Hungry is About to Hatch"*

Director – Gary Jones

Writer(s) – Stephen David Brooks / Jace Anderson / Adam Geirsach / Boaz Davidson

Starring – Lana Parrilla / Josh Green / Oliver Macready

Distributor – Nu Image Films

Released – Dec. 27, 2000.

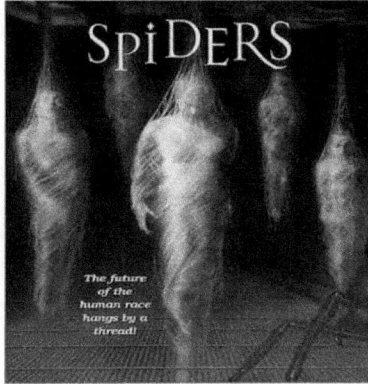

## Story:

A journalist, and two of her friends, investigate a crashed space shuttle and discovered a giant spider—which tries to kill them, of course.

## Cool Stuff:

Gary Jones also directed *Mosquito* (1995), *Crocodile 2: Death Swamp* (2002), *Ghouls* (2008), and *Ballistica* (2009).

Boaz Davidson has written many film stories—including *American Cyborg: Steel Warrior* (1993), *Crocodile* (2000), *Octopus* (2000), *Alien Hunter* (2003), *Snakeman* (2005), *SharkMan* (2005), and *Mega Snake* (2007). Anyone seeing a theme?

Lana Parrilla went on to star as Regina Mills (aka The Evil Queen) in the popular TV series *Once Upon A Time* (2011-17).

## TAIL STING (2001)

*"Don't Fasten Your Seatbelt!"*

Director – Paul Wynne

Writer(s) – Timothy Griffin / Peter Soby Jr.

Starring – Robert Merrill / Laura Putney

Distributor – Starmedia Home entertainment

Released – Jan. 1, 2001

*Story:*

Killer scorpions—on a plane.

*Cool Stuff:*

Paul Wynne also directed *El Chupacabra* (2003).

Laura Putney has appeared in such TV series as *JAG* (2002-03) and *ACME Saturday Night* (2009-11).

Robert Merrill went on to appear in several TV series—*Complete Works* (2014) and *Chasing Life* (2014-15).

Kevin McCarthy has been in the special effects business for many years, having worked on such films as—*The Return of the Living Dead* (1985), *Assault of the Killer Bimbos* (1988), *Waxwork II: Lost in Time* (1991), *Ice Cream Man* (1995), and the TV series *Monsters* (1989).

## SPIDERS II: BREEDING GROUND (2001)

*"They're Back...and This Time They're Breeding Mad!"*

Director – Sam Firstenberg

Writer(s) – Stephen David Brooks / Boaz Davidson

Starring – Stephanie Niznik / Greg Cromer / Richard Moll

Distributor – Nu Image Films

Released – May 9, 2001

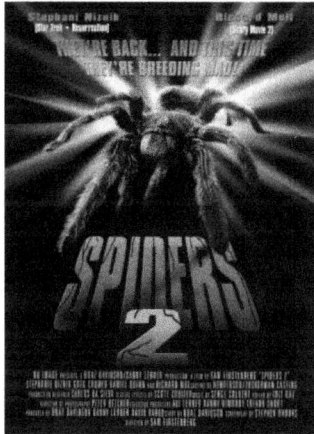

*Story:*

A giant spider terrorizes the crew of a ship.

*Cool Stuff:*

The film has no connection to the 2000 film *Spiders*—except the title and that the story was written by Boaz Davidson.

Sam Firstenberg also directed *Cyborg Cop* (1993) and *Blood Warriors* (1993).

Stephanie Niznik starred in the long-running TV series *Everwood* (2002-06).

Richard Moll is best known for his role as Bull on the TV series *Night Court* (1984-92). He has appeared in nearly 200 films/TV shows.

Daniel Quinn appeared in Scanner Cop (1994) and recent cult classic *Rubber* (2010).

## ARACHNID (2001)

*"It's Coming From Another World...To Stay!"*

Director – Jack Sholder

Writer(s) – Mark Sevi

Starring – Alex Reid / Chris Potter / Jose Sancho

Distributor – Lions Gate Films

Released – June 29, 2001

*Story:*

A group of researchers travel to Guam, looking for the cause of strange bites on a man who had been brought to a local clinic. But, when the plane they are on crashes, they soon discover the cause of the bites—a giant breed of killer spiders.

*Cool Stuff:*

Jack Sholder also directed *A Nightmare on Elm Street 2: Freddy's Revenge* (1985), *Wishmaster 2: Evil Never Dies* (1999), and *12 Days of Terror* (2004).

Mark Sevi has written numerous genre films, such as *Ghoulies IV (*1994), *Scanner Cop II* (1995), *Sci-Fighters* (1996), and *Pterodactyl* (2005).

Chris potter is also voiced Gambit in animated series *X-Men* (1992-96) and *Spider-Man* (1996).

Alex Reid appeared as Beth in the Horror classic, *The Descent* (2005).

**MIMIC 2 (2001)**

*"This time, nothing can stop it!"*

Director – Jean de Sesonzac

Writer(s) – Joel Soisson (based on a story by Donald A. Wollheim)

Starring – Alix Koromzay / Bruno Campos / Will Estes / Edward Albert

Distributor – Dimension Films

Released – July 17, 2001

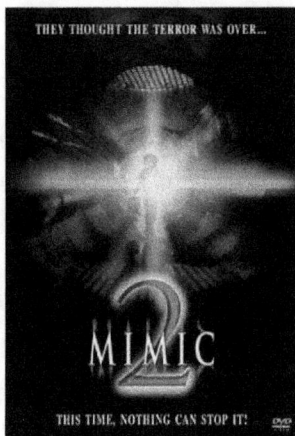

## Story:

The cockroach/human hybrids are back. A new team takes them on.

## Cool Stuff:

The film was a straight-to-DVD release.

Alix Koromzay has appeared in *The Haunting* (1999) and *Children of the Corn 666: Isaac's Return* (1999).

Will Estes had a small role in *The Dark Knight Rises* (2012).

Joe Polito is a character actor supreme, and has been in over 200 movies and TV series, such as *C.H.U.D.*

(1984), The Rocketeer (1991), *Tale of the Mummy* (1998), and *The Chronicle* (2001-02).

Michael Tucci is probably best remembered as Sonny in the movie, *Grease* (1978).

## EIGHT-LEGGED FREAKS (2002)

*"Let The Squashing Begin!"*

Director – Ellory Elkayem

Writer(s) – Ellory Elkayem / Jesse Alexander / based on a story by Ellory Elkayem & Randy Kornfield

Starring – David Arquette / Kari Wuhrer / Scarlett Johansson / Scott Terra / Doug E. Doug

Distributor – Warner Bros. Pictures

Released – July 17, 2002

*Story:*

Hometown boy, Chris McCormick (David Arquette) returns home after a ten-year absence. The town has called a meeting to decide if they want to sell the mine, and the residents to relocate. McCormick opposes the idea, and meeting becomes an argument over what is better for the town.

While the town argues over what to do, Sheriff Sam Parker (Kari Wuhrer), and Deputy Pete Williams (Rick Overton) find barrels of toxic waste in a local pond. Soon after, spiders that have been exposed to the toxic water, and are growing, begin an assault on the town.

The town becomes quickly overrun by giant spiders of all types, and the residents—who are still alive and able to fight—gather at the mall, where they become trapped by a swarm of giant spiders. McCormick, Parker, and several of the townspeople make their way to the mine, and finally destroys spiders' nest.

A mix of humor and quality CGI effects makes this a very fun film.


*Cool Stuff:*

The original title of the film was Arac Attack.

The film was produced by Dean Devlin and Roland Emmerich—who also produced *Stargate* (1994), and *Independence Day* (1996).

Kari Wuhrer appeared in the Sci-Fi series, *Sliders* (1995-2000), and such films as, *Anaconda* (1997), and *Hellraiser: Deader* (2005).

David Arquette is best known for portraying Dewey Riley in the *Scream* ( 1996-2011) film series.

A variety of spiders were used in the film—including tarantulas, jumping spiders, orb weavers, and trapdoor spiders.

The film is based on the short film, *Larger Than Life*, which director Ellory Elkayem created in 1997—for a film project.

The film is one of the early roles for the young Scarlett Johansson.

Rick Overton has been in numerous films, such as *Willow* (1988), *Groundhog Day* (1993), and *Cloverfield* (2008)

Frank Welker, who provides the sounds/voices of the queen spider, and other spider vocal effects, is also the voice of some well-known cartoon characters— Jabber Jaw, Megatron, and Freddy from Scooby-Doo.

**INFESTED (2002)**

*"Invasion of the Killer Bugs"*

Director – Josh Olson

Writer(s) – Josh Olsen

Starring – Zach Galligan / Lisa Ann Hadley / Daniel Jenkins / Any Jo Johnson

Distributor – Sony Pictures

Released – Oct. 18, 2002

*Story:*

When friends gather at a funeral, they are attacked by killer flies—whose bite turns people into zombies.

*Cool Stuff:*

John Olson is better known for writing the screenplay for *A History of Violence* (2005).

Zach Galligan has appeared in numerous genre films, such as *Gremlins* (1984), *Gremlin 2: The Next Batch* (1990), *Waxwork* (1988), *Waxwork II: Lost in Time* (1992), and *Warlock: The Armageddon* (1993).

Amy Jo Johnson is best known as The Pink Ranger in *Mighty Morphin Power Rangers* (1993-99) and Jules in the TV series *Flashpoint* (2008-12).

Max Ink Café was responsible for the special effects.

## WEBS (2003)

*"A Parallel Dimension...A Gateway to Hell."*

Director – David Wu

Writer(s) – Greenville Case

Starring – Richard Grieco / Richard Yearwood / Kate Greenhouse / Colin Fox

Distributor – Universal Pictures

Released – June 28, 2003

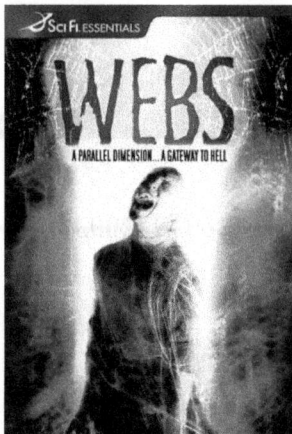

_Story:_

A crew of electricians end up in a parallel universe—which is ruled by giant spiders.

_Cool Stuff:_

Richard Grieco rose to fame as Office Dennis Booker on _21 Jump Street_ (1988-89).

Kate Greenhouse also appeared in the genre films _The Dark Hours_ (2005) and _He Never Died_ (2015).

Colin Fox has appeared in over 150 films and TV shows, including voice work for _The Legend of Zelda_ (1989), _Beetlejuice_ (1989), _Babar_ (1989-91), _Wild C.A.T.S: Covert Actions Teams_ (1994-95), and _Rupert_ (1991-97).

Richard Yearwood is a talented voice actor in such animated series as, _Monster Force_ (1994) and _Donkey Kong Country_ (1997-200). He has also appeared as Ganymede in _Percy Jackson: Sea of Monsters_ (2013).

**BUGS (2003)**

_"You Can't Kill What You Can't See."_

Director – Joseph Conti

Writer(s) – Robinson Young / Patrick J. Doody / Chris Valenziano / and Joe Conti

Starring – Antonio Sabato Jr. / Angie Everhart

Distributor – Sci-Fi Pictures

Released – Sept. 6, 2003

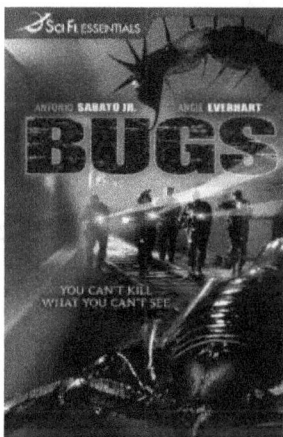

## Story:

An engineer, and an entomologist, are trapped in an underground tunnel—with giant scorpion-like monsters.

## Cool Stuff:

Joe Conti is best known for his visual effects work, in such films as *Men in Black* (1997), *The Siege* (1998), and *Army of the Dead* (2008).

Antonio Sabato Jr. is probably best known for his roles as Alonzo Solace on *Earth 2* (1994-95) and as Dante on the daytime TV series, *The Bold and the Beautiful* (2005-06).

Angie Everhart appeared as Lilith in *Bordello of Blood* (1996).

Robinson Young also wrote *Webs* (2003).

## MIMIC 3: SENTINEL (2003)

"Terror has been reinvented"

Director – J.T. Petty

Writer(s) – J.T. Petty (based on the story by Donald A. Wollheim)

Starring – Amanda Plummer / Karl Geary / Lance Henriksen / Alexis Dzeina

Distributor – Dimension Films

Released – Oct. 14, 2003

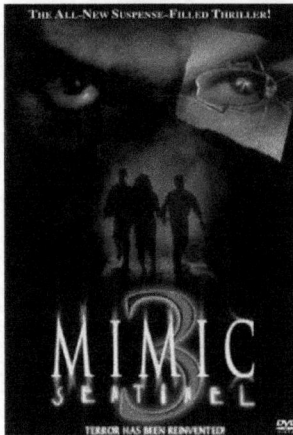

*Story:*

The cockroach/human hybrids are back for a third time, and an asthmatic photographer is the one who notices people in his neighborhood are going missing. He, and a small group of neighbors must the battle the creatures—if they want to survive.

*Cool Stuff:*

This was also released direct-to-DVD.

Karl Geary has appeared in *The Burrowers* (2008) and *I Am Not A Serial Killer* (2016).

Keith Robinson played the Green Lightpseed Ranger in several Power Rangers programs.

Amanda Plummer has been in many films, such as *The Fisher King* (1991) *and Needful Things* (1993).

Rebecca Mader poatrayed Dr. Charlotte Staples Lewis on the TV series, *Lost* (2008-10).

Veteran act John Kapelos has appeared in *Forever Knight* (1992-95) and *The Shape of Water* (2017).

## THE BONE SNATCHER (2003)

*"It will scare you out of your skull"*

Director – Jason Wulfsohn

Writer(s) – Malcolm Kohll / Gordon Render

Starring – Scott Bairstow / Rachel Shelley / Patrick Lyster / Adrienne Pierce

Distributor – Overseas FilmGroup

Released – Dec. 23, 2003

## Story:

After miners begin disappearing, a group of geologists travel to South Africa to investigate. They soon find themselves battling for their lives—against a swarm of ant-like creatures.

## Cool Stuff:

It was filmed in the deserts of Namibia and the city of Cape Town, South Africa.

# CENTIPEDE! (2004)

*"Deep In The Earth Terror Awaits"*

Director – Gregory Gieras

Writer(s) – Gregory Gieras

Starring – Larry Casey / Margaret Cash / Trevor Murphy

Distributor – Generon Entertainment

Released – Nov. 6, 2004

## Story:

A group of spelunkers travel to India to explore a cave. An earthquake traps them underground—where they encounter giant killer centipedes.

## Cool Stuff:

Gregory Gieras wrote *Dark Island* (2010) and *Big Ass Spider!* (2013).

This is the only film credit for actress Margaret Cash.

Many of the cast and crew of this film no longer work in the industry—or have any other credits to their name.

**SWARMED (2005)**

*"Man Doesn't Rule the Planet Anymore"*

Director – Paul Ziller

Writer – Miquel Tejada-Flores

Starring – Michael Shanks / Carol Alt / Richard Chevolleau / Tim Thomerson

Distributor – Sci-Fi Pictures

Released – April 6, 2005

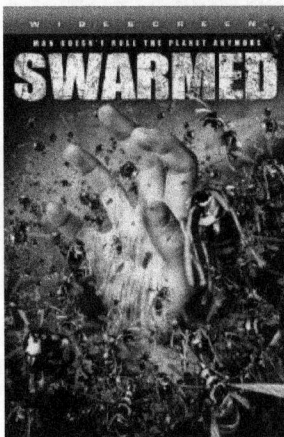

## Story:

A scientist creates a super pesticide that accidently produces a swarm of killer yellow jackets, He then must lead the battle when the wasps begin to terrorize his small town.

## Cool Stuff:

Paul Ziller also directed *Snakehead Terror* (2004), *Solar Attack* (2006), *Android Apocalypse* (2006), *Yeti: Curse of the Snow Demon* (2008), and *Iron Golem* (2011).

Miquel Tejada-Flores has written numerous films— including *Revenge of the Nerds* (1984), *Screamers* (1995), *Beyond Re-Animator* (2003), and *Frankenstein's Army* (2013).

Michael Shanks is probably best known for his portrayal as Dr. Daniel Jackson on *Stargate SG-1* (1997-2007).

Carol Alt was one of the top models of the 1980s.

Richard Chevolleu played Augur on the TV series, *Earth: Final Conflict* (1997-2001).

## GLASS TRAP (2005)

*"There's No Escape"*

Director – Fred Olen Ray (as Ed Raymond)

Writer(s) – Lisa Morton / Brett Thompson

Starring – C. Thomas Howell / Stella Stevens / Siri Baruc / Andrew Pine

Distributor – First Look Home Entertainment

Released – Aug. 2, 2005

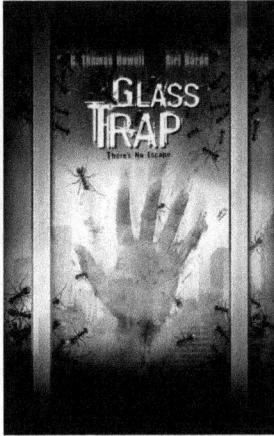

## Story:

Radioactive ants terrorize a group of people, in a skyscraper.

## Cool Stuff:

C. Thomas Howell has been in over 200 movies—including such genre classics as *E.T. The Extra-Terrestrial* (1982) and *The Hitcher* (1986).

Andrew Pine has been in nearly 200 films, including *The Town That Dreaded Sundown* (1976), *Amityville II: The Possession* (1982), *Eliminators* (1986), and the TV series *Weird Science* (1994-98).

Siri Baruc also appeared in *The Wisher* (2002), *Mega Snake* (2007) and *Unholy* (2007).

The film was co-written by Horror writer, Lisa Morton.

Director Fed Olen Ray is a film icon, having produced/directed/written such classics as— *Hollywood Chainsaw Hookers* (1988), *Evil Toons* (1992), *Attack of the 60 Foot Centerfold (*1995), and the TV series, *The Lair* (2007-09).

## INSECTICIDAL (2005)

*"These Girls Have A New Major...Survival"*

Director – Jeffrey Lando

Writer(s) – Jeff O'Brien

Starring – Meghan Heffren / Travis Watters

Distributor – Shoreline Entertainment

Released – Oct. 22, 2005

*Story:*

Sorority girls battle giant bugs.

*Cool Stuff:*

Jeffrey Scott Lando has also directed a handful of TV movies—*House of Bones* (2010), *Goblin* (2010), *Boogeyman* (2012), and *Roboshark* (2015).

Meghan Heffren also starred in the remake of *The Fog* (2005), and *The Shrine* (2010).

Travis Watters starred in *American Mary* (2012).

Samantha McLeod has also been in *Snakes on a Plane* (2006).

# LOCUSTS: THE 8th PLAGUE (2005)

*"Watch The Skies…And Run!"*

Director – Ian Gilmour

Writer(s) – D.R. Rosen

Starring – Dan Cortese / David Keith / Julie Benz / Jeff Fahey

Distributor – MGM

Released – Nov. 12, 2005

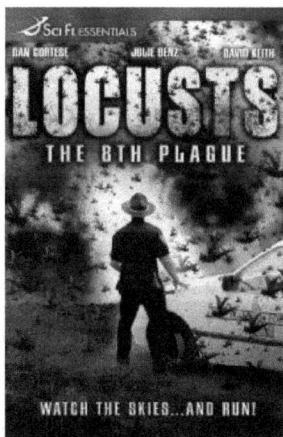

### Story:

Genetically mutated locusts—that consume living flesh—escape from a lab and terrorize a group of Idaho farmers.

### Cool Stuff:

Ian Gilmour directed episodes of *Beastmaster* (1999-2001) and *The Lost World* (2000-02).

Jeff Fahey is well-known to genre film fans. He has starred in over 150 films, such as—*The Lawnmower Man* (1992), *Serpent's Lair* (1995), *Epicenter* (2000), *Darkhunters* (2004), *Planet Terror* (2007), and *Machete* (2010).

Veteran actor, David Keith, has starred in many films, including—*Firestarter* (1984), *U-571* (2000), *Epoch* (2001), and *Sabretooth* (2002).

Dan Cortese is probably best known for his role on the long-running TV series, *Veronica's Closet* (1997-2000).

## CAVED IN (2006)

*"The Ultimate Threat. The Gravest Danger. Hidden in the Earth"*

Director – Richard Pepin

Writer(s) – Neil Elman

Starring – Christopher Atkins / Colm Meaney / Angela Featherstone / Monica Barladeanu

Distributor – CineTel Films

Released – January 7, 2006

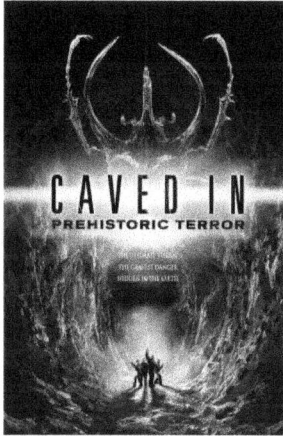

*Story:*

A group of thieves, searching for emeralds in a Switzerland mine, encounter giant rhinoceros beetles—that try to kill them.

*Cool Stuff:*

Colm Meaney is best known for portraying Miles O'Brien on *Star Trek: The Next Generation* and Star Trek: Deep Space Nine.

Christopher Atkins achieved a brief moment of fame when appeared opposite Brooke Shields in *The Blue Lagoon* (1980).

Richard Pepin also directed *The Sender* (1998), *Mindstorm* (2001) and *The Box* (2003).

# SLITHER (2006)

*"Horror Has A New Face."*

Director – James Gunn

Writer(s) – James Gunn

Starring – Nathan Fillion / Elizabeth Banks / Michael Rooker

Distributor – Universal Pictures

Released – Mar. 31, 2006

## Story:

A meteorite crashes into the forest near a small South Carolina town. Grant (Michael Rucker) runs into the alien parasite that has escaped from the meteorite—and it begins to change him. His wife, Starla (Elizabeth Banks) notices the change in his personality—and face—and calls police chief, Bill

Pardy (Nathan Fillion). Meanwhile, pets in the area begin to disappear.

Having infected his mistress, Brenda (Brenda James), Grant hides her in a barn—where she begins to transform into a gigantic egg sack. When Pardy and his fellow officers eventually find her, but she explodes, and the alien slugs attack the group—infecting them. The infected begin munching on others in the community.

Pardy leads a ragtag group to find Grant, who is trying to find his wife—so he can turn her. They eventually find him just before he can change his wife. And we are given a splattering good ending. Or is it the end?

### Cool Stuff:

James Gunn went on to write and direct two little films titled, *Guardians of the Galaxy* (2104) and *Guardians of the Galaxy: Vol. 2* (2017). He also wrote the screenplay for the remake of *Dawn of the Dead* (2004), and made the dark superhero film, *Super* (2010).

Nathan Fillion played Captain Mal Reynolds on the cult series, *Firefly* (2002-03) and its film sequel, *Serenity* (2005), and starred in the long running series, *Castle* (2009-16). He is also a popular voice actor, having voiced Green Lantern in the animated film, *Green Lantern: Emerald Knights* (2011) and *Justice League: Doom* (2012), and characters on *Robot Chicken (2007-14).*

Elizabeth Banks has appeared in many films—Sam Raimi's *Spider-Man* trilogy (2002-07), *The Hunger Games* series (2012-15), and the TV series *30 Rock* (2010-12).

Fan favorite Michael Rooker can be found in *The Dark Half* (1993), *The Trigger Effect* (1996), and *Jumper* (2008), But, he is best known as Merle Dixon on *The Walking Dead* (2010-13) and Yondu in *Guardian of the Galaxy* films (2014 / 2017).

Don Thompson can also be seen in such popular TV series as, *Blade: The Series* (2006), *Battlestar Galactica* (2005-09), and *The Killing* (2011-12).

Jenna Fischer is the wife of director James Gunn.

Nathan Fillion was cast just one week before filming began.

The voice of Dr. Karl—who talks to Starla on the phone—is Rob Zombie.

Cinematographer, Gregory Middleton, has also worked on the TV series, *Fringe* (2010-11), *The Killing* (2012-14), and *Game of Thrones* (2015-17).

John Gajdecki has supervised visual effects for many TV series—*War of the Worlds* (1989-90), *Beyond Reality* (1991-92), *The Outer Limits* (1995), and *Van Helsing* (2016).

Todd Masters has done makeup effects for *Leprechaun 2* (1994), *Monster Man* (2003), *Snakes on a Plane* (2006), and the TV series *Tales from the Crypt* (1992-95) and *Carnivale* (2003).

## ICE SPIDERS (2007)

*"Hell Has Just Frozen Over"*

Director - Tibor Takacs

Writer(s) – Eric Miller

Starring – Patrick Muldoon / Vanessa A. Williams / Thomas Calabro

Distributor – Regent Worldwide

Released – June 9, 2007

### Story:

The government has created a breed of giant, deadly spiders. Of course, the spiders escape and terrorize a ski resort filled with Olympic skiers.

*Cool Stuff:*

Tibor Takacs also directed *The Gate* (1987), *Rats* (2003), and *Mega Snake* (2007).

Patrick Muldoon is probably best known for his role as Zander Barcalow in *Starship Troopers* (1997), but also appeared in *Arrival II* (1998), *Stigmata* (1999).

Vanessa Williams is a prominent TV actress, having starred in several long-running TV shows—such as *Melrose Place* (1992-93), *Murder One* (1995-96), and *Soul Food* (2000-04).

Thomas Calabro starred in another killer bug movie, *They Nest* (2000) aka *Creepy Crawlers* (2001).

Charles Halford portrayed Agent Shaw on *Agents of S.H.I.E.L.D.* (2013-14) and Chas Chandler on the TV series *Constantine* (2014-15).

**IN THE SPIDER'S WEB (2007)**

*"Caught in the Web of Fear"*

Director – Terry Winsor

Writer(s) – Gary Dauberman

Starring – Lance Henriksen / Emma Catherwood / Lisa Livingstone / Cian Barry

Distributor – RHI Entertainment / Genius Entertainment

Released – August 2007

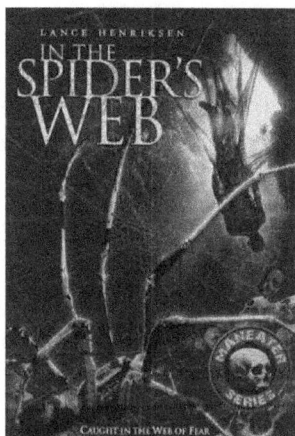

*Story:*

A group of American backpackers, traveling across India, seek out an American doctor living in the jungle—after one of them is bitten by a spider.

Of course, Doctor Lecorpus (Lance Henriksen) has been harvesting traveler's organs and the spider's venom helps the organs remain unspoiled.

It soon becomes a fight for the backpacker's lives as they battle killer spiders, Dr. Lecorpus, and the native population.

*Cool Stuff:*

Lance Henriksen is a genre film legend, having starred in classics like *Aliens* (1986), *Pumpkinhead* (1988), and the TV series, *Millennium* (1996-99).

Emma Catherwood also appeared in *The Reeds* (2010).

Lisa Livingstone can be seen in The Redwood Massacre (2014) and the TV Mini-Series, *The Loch* (2017).

Jane Perry does voice work for many video games—such as *Hitman: Absolution* (2012), *Dreamfall Chapters* (2014), *Soma* (2105), *Mass Effect: Andromeda* (2017), and also starred in *The Autopsy of Jane Doe* (2016) and *The Beyond* (2017).

This is Gary Dauberman's first tv/film writing credit. He then went on to write *Annabelle* (2014), *Within* (2016), *It* (2017), and is working on *It: Chapter Two* (2019) and the TV series *Swamp Thing* (2019).

The film is part of a trilogy of films under the "Maneaters Series collection"—which was released in 2008.

## DESTINATION: INFESTATION (2007)

*"You Will be Infected"*

Director – George Mendeluk

Writer(s) – Mary Weinstein

Starring – Jessalyn Gilsis / Serge Houde / Antonio Sabato Jr.

Distributor – A&E

Resale – July 7, 2007

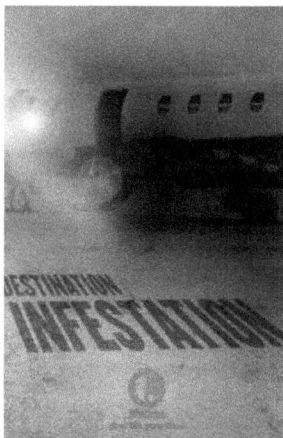

*Story:*

Passengers on a plane vs. poisonous ants.

*Cool Stuff:*

George Mendeluk directed episodes of such TV series as—*Hercules: The Legendary Journeys* (1995), *The Adventures of Sinbad* (1996-98), and *Highlander: The Raven* (1998-99).

Jessalyn Gilsig went on to play the role of Siggy Haraldson in the series, *Vikings* (2013-15).

Antonio Sabato Jr. is probably best known for his long-running role as Dante Damiano in the daytime soap opera, *The Bold and The Beautiful* (2005-06).

Serge Houde appears on the TV series, *iZombie* (2015-17).

## BLACK SWARM (2007)

*"If You Can See The Swarm…It's Too Late"*

Director – David Winning

Writer(s) – Todd Samovitz / Ethlie Ann Vare

Starring – Sebastien Roberts / Sarah Allen / Robert Englund

Distributor – Genius Entertainment

Released – Dec. 7, 2007

### Story:

Sheriff Jane Kozik (Sarah Allen), a recent widow, moves Black Stone, New York—with her daughter Kelsey (Rebecca Windheim). When the body of a homeless man is found in a neighbor's shed, Jane enlists the help of entomologist Katherine Randell (Jayne Heitmeyer) and Devin Hall (Sebastein Roberts) to find out why. Their investigation finds that the army has created super-wasps to use as a weapon. Of course, the wasps escape and begin terrorizing Black Stone—and out group must find a way to stop them.

## *Cool Stuff:*

David Winning is a genre veteran, having directed episodes of *Are You Afraid of the Dark?* (1993-95), *Earth: Final Conflict* (2001-02), and *Andromeda* (2000-05).

Sarah Allen has appeared in the TV series, *Murdock Mysteries* (2009) and *Being Human* (2011-14).

Jayne Heitmeyer is probably best known for her portrayal of Lt. Briony Branca on *NightMan* (1998-99) and Renee Palmer on *Earth: Final Conflict* (1999-2002).

Robert Englund—well, if you don't know he played Freddy Kruger in the *Nightmare on Elm Street* film series, I'm sorry.

Todd Samovitz also wrote *Wonderland* (2003).

Ethlie Ann Vare has written for many genre projects, such as the TV series *Earth: Final Conflict* (1998-2000) and *Andromeda* (2000-02),

## THE HIVE (2008)

*"Death Is Their Picnic."*

Director – Peter Manus

Writer(s) – T.S. Cook

Starring – Tom Wopat / Elizabeth Healey / Kal Weber

Distributor – RHI Entertainment

Released – Feb. 17, 2008

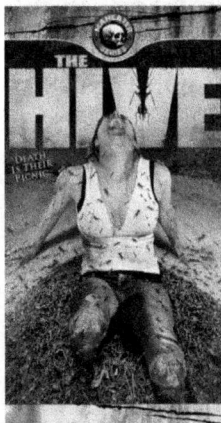

### Story:

The Thorax Company is called to a small Brazilian island to exterminate an army of flesh-eating ants. When they arrive, they discover that the ants can communicate with us—and they have decided they want control of the island. Or, is something else controlling the ants?

## Cool Stuff:

Tom Wopat is best known as Luke Duke from the popular TV series, *The Dukes of Hazzard* (1979-85).

Elizabeth Healey has also appeared in the TV series, *The Fugitives* (2005) and a small role in *Doctor Strange* (2016).

Kevin Chisnall has done special effects for such films as *Willow* (1988), *Croc* (2007), and *The Scorpion King 3* (2012).

## STAR RUNNERS (2009)

Director – Mat King

Writer – Rafael Jordan

Starring – Conner Trinneer / Toni Trucks

Distributor – Sci-Fi Channel

Released – June 13, 2009

_Story:_

The crew of a crashed spaceship battles alien insects.

_Cool Stuff:_

Mat King directed episodes of _Spirit Warriors_ (2010) and _Doctor Who_ (2013).

Rafael Jordon has written many TV movies, including _Thor: Hammer of the Gods_ (2009), _Meteor Storm_ (2010), _Dragon Wasps_ (2012), _Cowboys vs Dinosaurs_ (2015).

Connor Trinneer is best known for his role as Commander "Trip" Tucker III on the TV series, _Star Trek: Enterprise_ (2001-05).

James Kyson starred as Ando Masahashi in _Heroes_ (2006-10), as well as appearing in _Blade of Honor_ (2017) and _Preacher_ (2017).

Mat King has directed episodes of _Spirit Warriors_ (2010) and _Doctor Who_ (2012)

## HIGH PLAINS INVADERS (2009)

*"No One Invited Them. Nothing Can Stop Them."*

Director – K.T. Donaldson (Kristoffer Tabori)

Writer – Richard Beattie

Starring – James Marsters / Cindy Sampson / Sebastian Knapp

Distributor – SyFy Channel

Released – Aug. 30, 2009

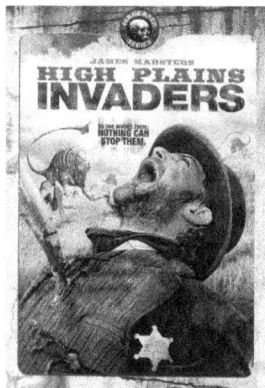

### Story:

When alien insect-like creatures arrive in a small wild west town, the townsfolks must join forces with a band of outlaws to fight the monsters.

## Cool Stuff:

James Marsters is best known as the cool vampire, Spike, on the series *Buffy, The Vampire Slayer* (1997-2003) and *Angel* (1999-2004).

Cindy Sampson played Lisa Braeden on *Supernatural* (2007-11) and starred in *The Shrine* (2010).

Marie-Eve Bedard-Tremblay also coordinated the visual effects for such films as—*Source Code* (2011), *Star Trek Beyond* (2016) and the TV series *Being Human* (2011-14).

Director Kristoffer Tabori (as K.T. Donaldson), has also directed for numerous TV shows—like *Bill & Ted's Excellent Adventures* (1992), *Profiler* (1998-99), and *Judging Amy* (2000-01).

## INFESTATION (2009)

*"Prepare For Global Swarming"*

Director – Kyle Rankin

Writer – Kyle Rankin

Starring - Chris Marquette / Brooke Nevin / Ray Wise

Distributor – Icon Productions

Released – Nov. 21, 2009

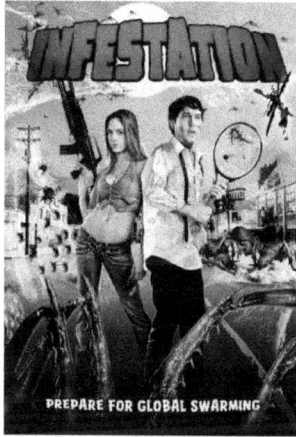

PREPARE FOR GLOBAL SWARMING

## Story:

Telemarketer, Cooper (Chris Marquette) is fired one morning for showing up late—again. After leaving the building, he hears a strange buzzing sound and collapses. When he wakes up, he is cocooned inside his former office. Breaking free, he is attacked by a giant bug, but manages to escape and finds his boss, Maureen (Deborah Geffner) and her daughter Sara (Brooke Nevin)—whom he rescues from cocoons, as well. Unfortunately, Maureen is attacked and taken away by a giant flying bug.

The duo run to a nearby restaurant, where they meet another group of people hiding from the bugs. They try to escape, but many are killed. The remaining group find their way to the home of Ethan (Ray Wise)—a former soldier that just happens to have a slew of weapons.

Sara is captured by some bugs and taken to their hive—where she sees people being eaten by the bug queen. Cooper, Ethan, and a new companion, Hugo (E. Quincy Sloan) arrive to save Sara. Ethan begins to turn into a human/bug hybrid and gives Cooper a remote to trigger explosives he had planted—and hopefully killing the alien bugs.

## Cool Stuff:

Chris Marquette also starred in the TV series, *The Mummy: Secrets of the Medjai* (2001-03), as well as *Freddy vs. Jason* (2003), *The Girl Next Door* (2004), and *Alpha Dog* (2006).

Brooke Nevin played Rachel Berenson on the TV series, *Animorphs* (19988-99) and Nikki Hudson on *The 4400* (2004-06).

Veteran actor, Ray Wise, has starred in numerous genre films—including *Robocop* (1987), and *Jeepers Creepers II* (2003), but is probably best known for playing Leland Palmer in the cult TV classic, *Twin Peaks* (1990-91).

Deborah Geffner appeared in *All That Jazz* (1979), *Star 80* (1983) and *Exterminator 2* (1984).

Linda Park is best known for her portrayal of Hoshi Sato on *Star Trek: Enterprise* (2001-05).

Kyle Rankin also directed *Night of the Living Deb* (2015).

Efram Potelle created special effects for *Punisher: War Zone* (2008), *Wrong Turn 4: Bloody Beginnings*

(2011), and several episodes of *Agents of S.H.I.E.L.D.* (2015).

## CAMEL SPIDERS (2011)

*"They Really Get Under Your Skin"*

Director – Jim Wynorski

Writer(s) – J. Brad Wilke / Jim Wynorski

Starring – Brian Krause / Melissa Brasselle / C. Thomas Howell

Distributor – SyFy / Anchor Bay Entertainment

Released – Mar. 4, 2011

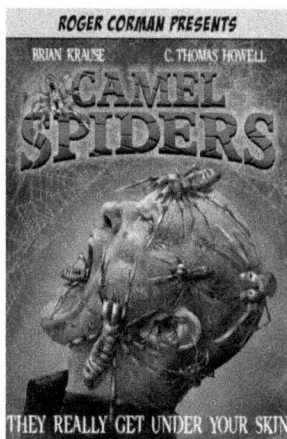

*Story:*

Camel spiders—having traveled back with U.S. soldiers returning from the Middle East—begin terrorizing the southwest United States.

## Cool Stuff:

Jim Wynorski has directed over a hundred films, including *Chopping Mall* (1986*), Deathstalker II* (1987), *Dinosaur Island* (1994), and *Komodo vs. Cobra* (2005).

Actors would switch from American soldier uniforms to Taliban uniforms—after lunch.

Brian Krause is probably best known for playing Leo Wyatt on *Charmed* (1998-2006).

C. Thomas Howell has been in film since childhood, having starred in *E.T. the Extra-Terrestrial* (1982), *The Outsiders* (1983), *The Hitcher* (1986), *The Glass Jar* (1999) and the TV series, *Amazon* (1999-2000).

Melissa Brasselle has also starred in *Raptor* (2001), *The Curse of the Komodo* (2004), and *Vampire in Vegas* (2009).

Jon Mack has appeared in *Saw VI* (2009), *Mongolian Death Worm* (2010), and *Spiders 3-D* (2013).

**ARACHNOQUAKE (2012)**

Director – G.E. Furst

Writer(s) – Paul A. Birkett / Eric Forsberg

Starring – Megan Adelle / Gralen Bryant Banks /
Edward Furlong / Tracey Gold

Distributor – Syfy

Released – June 23, 2012

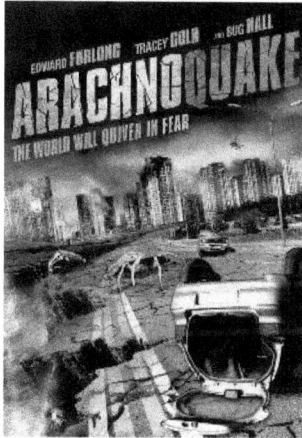

## Story:

An earthquake unleashes giant, fire-breathing spiders
on the city of New Orleans.

## Cool Stuff:

Director, Griff Furst is primarily and actor, having
starred in *Boa vs Python* (2004), *Dracula's Curse*
(2006), *Monsterwolf* (2010), and *Devil's Due* (2013).

Eric Forsberg has written a handful of films, such as *Alien Abduction* (2005), *Snakes on A Train* (2006) and *Mega Piranha* (2010).

Tracy Gold is best known for her role as Carol Seaver on *Growing Pains* (1985-92).

Edward Furlong's more famous roles as John Conner in *Terminator 2: Judgment Day* (1991) and Danny Vinyard in *American History X* (1998).

P.J. Foley also did special effects for such films Locusts: *The 8th Plague* (2005), *Reign of the Gargoyles* (2007) and *Anaconda: The Offspring* (2008).

The film only took 17 days to shoot.

### DRAGON WASPS (2012)

*"A New Breed of Evil"*

Director – Joe Knee

Writer(s) – Mark Atkins / Rafael Jordan

Starring – Corin Nemec / Dominika Julliet / Nikolette Noel / Benjamin Easterday

Distributor – SyFy Channel / American World Pictures

Released – Dec. 1, 2012

## Story:

When her father disappears in the jungles of Belize, a scientist asks the US Army for help finding him. When they arrive, they encounter giant wasps.

## Cool Stuff:

Writer Mark Artkins is also a cinematographer, where he worked on *Snakes on a Train* (2006), *Halloween Night* (2006), and *2012: Supernova* (2009).

Corin Nemec is best known for his role as Parker Lewis on *Parker Lewis Can't Lose* (1990-93) and Jonas Quinn on *Stargate SG-1* (2002-04).

Vanessa Evigan is and visual effects producer.

# SPIDERS 3D (2013)

*"The City is Crawling"*

Director – Tibor Takacs

Writer(s) – Joseph Farrugia / Tibor Takacs / Boaz Davidson / Dustin Warburton

Starring – Patrick Muldoon / Christ Campbell

Distributor – Nu Image

Released – Feb. 8, 2013

## Story:

A Russian space station falls to earth and crashes into a New York subway tunnel. A NY Transit worker, Jason (Patrick Muldoon) sends his coworker to investigate the damage. When the man is found dead—and covered in strange bite marks—Jason calls his ex-wife, and coroner, Rachel (Christa Campbell) to help him find out what happened. She finds eggs inside the man's body.

Hazmat workers also descend into the tunnels to look for any radiation. Though they declare the area safe, in another part of the tunnel, some homeless men are found—covered in spider webs. Authorities enforce a quarantine.

Jason and Rachel soon find out that the Russians had discovered an alien spaceship in the ice some 20 years ago. They had taken the genes of the aliens and injected them into a variety of creatures. Only spiders survived and the queen could produce bulletproof strength webbing—which they hoped to use for military purposes. They were carrying out studies on the space station.

As expected, The Russian scientists try to recover the queen, while Jason and Rachel attempt to kill it.

### Cool Stuff:

Tibor Takacs also directed *The Gate* (1987), *I, Madman* (1989), *Rats* (2003), *Mansquito* (2005) and *Ice Spiders* (2007).

William Hope has appeared in numerous films, including *Aliens* (1986), *xXx* (2002), *Sherlock Holmes* (2009) and *Captain America: The First Avenger* (2011).

Patrick Muldoon is best known for his role as Zander Barcalow in *Starship Troopers* (1997).

Christa Campbell also appeared in *Day of the Dead* (2008) and *Drive Angry* (2011).

Sydney Sweeney stars in Hulu series, *The Handmaid's Tale* (2018).

David Lobato did special effects for *Fast Five* (2011), *The Hobbit: Desolation of Smaug* (2013), *Batman v Superman: Dawn of Justice* (2016), and episodes of *Terminator: The Sarah Conner Chronicles* (2008-09) and *Game of Thrones* (2015).

## BIG ASS SPIDER! (2013)

*"10 Stories High…and Very Hungry"*

Director – Mike Mendez

Writer(s) – Gregory Gieras

Starring – Greg Grunberg / Clare Kramer / Lin Shaye / Lombardo Boyar / Ray Wise

Distributor – Paramount Pictures

Released – Oct. 18, 2013

*Story:*

After being bitten by a spider, an exterminator named Alex (Greg Grunberg), is taken to a hospital for treatment. While there, a rat-sized spider climbs out of a dead body and bites the mortician. Alex agrees to deal with the spider problem, in exchange for the hospital paying for his bill.

While searching for the spider, the military shows up to examine the dead body. Lieutenant Karly Brant (Clare Kramer), and a hospital security guard, Jose (Lombardo Boyar) help Alex in his search—which leads them outside, where they find the spider, which growing larger by the minute, has killed a homeless man and is heading into the city.

The spider continues to grow larger until it is gigantic. It soon begins to terrorize the people of L.A., and the military begins an assault on the creature. Alex and Jose eventually confront the giant spider head-on, and Alex uses a rocket launcher and shoots the spider in its spinneret—blowing the spider up—and saving the city.

## Cool Stuff:

Director Mike Mendez could not afford a casting director, so he used some of his Facebook friends. He also directed *The Convent* (2000), and *The Gravedancers* (2006).

Greg Grunberg was also in the TV series, *Heroes* (2006-2010), and *Heroes Reborn* (2015).

Clare Kramer is probably best known to fans as Glory, on the TV series, *Buffy the Vampire Slayer* (1997-2003).

Lin Shaye has been in nearly 200 films, including such genre classics as—*A Nightmare on Elm Street* (1984), *Critters* (1986), *The Running Man* (1987), *2001 Maniacs* (2005), *Insidious* (2010), and *Tales of Halloween* (2015). She is also sister to Robert Shaye.

Lombardo Boyar has appeared in *The Bernie Mac Show* (2001-06) and *Dawn of the Planet of the Apes* (2014). He is also the voice of Raul in the *Happy Feet* franchise.

Patrick Bauchau is probably best known for his roles as Sydney on *The Pretender* (19996-2000) and Professor Ernst Lodz on *Carnivale* (2003-05).

The jogger was played by Lloyd Kaufman—of Troma Films.

A mid-credit scene shows a giant cockroach climbing the Statue of Liberty.

## ARACHNICIDE (2014)

*"Arachnicide or Die!"*

Director – Paolo Bertola

Writer(s) – Paolo Bertola / Ruben Maria Soriquez

Starring – Gabriel Cash / Gino Barzacchi / Mark Dodson

Distributor – Midnight Releasing / Brain Damage Film

Released – April 2014

### Story:

A Special Forces Unit named L9 Commando fights giant killer spiders—a result of years of genetic manipulation.

*Cool Stuff:*

Director Paolo Bertola also served as film editor and special effects supervisor.

It was filmed under the working title, *L9 Commando*.

## LAVALANTULA (2015)

*"Fire Burns...Lava Bites"*

Director – Mike Mendez

Writer(s) – Neil Elman / Ashley O'Neil

Starring – Steve Guttenberg / Nia Peebles

Distributor – Cinetel Films / SyFy

Released – July 25, 2015

*Story:*

A washed-up 90's action star, Colton West (Steve Guttenberg) is forced to appeared in low-budget horror films to pay the bills. Stuck in traffic one afternoon, a series of earthquakes shake Southern California—at the same time a volcano erupts in the Santa Monica Mountains. The convergence of natural forces also brings lava-spewing tarantulas to the surface, where they begin attacking the populace.

Colton must use his former—fake—action star skills to find his family. With the help of several film friends, they face off against the deadly spiders. Action and silliness ensues.

*Cool Stuff:*

Four *Police Academy* (1984) veterans star in the film.

Steve Guttenberg starred in four *Police Academy* films, as well as *Short Circuit* (1986) and *3 Men and A Baby* (1987).

Michael Winslow is a talented voice actor, who also starred in six *Police Academy* films.

Marion Ramsey starred in six *Police Academy* films, as well as *The Addams Family* TV series (1992-93).

Nia Peeples is probably best known for her role as Nicole Chapman on *Fame* (1983-86) and Sydney Cooke on *Walker, Texas Ranger* (1999-2001).

Ian Ziering guest-stars as Fin Shepard—*Sharknado*.

Mike Mendez also wrote and/or directed *The Gravedancers* (2003), *Big Ass Spider!* (2013), *Tales of Halloween* (2015).

Neil Elman also wrote *Mongolian Death Worm* (2010), *I Spit on You Grave 2* (2013), and *They Found Hell* (2015).

## STUNG (2015)

*"The Ultimate Buzzkill"*

Director – Benni Diez

Writer(s) – Adam Aresty

Starring – Matt O'Leary / Jessica Cook

Distributor – IFC Midnight

Release Date – July 3, 2015

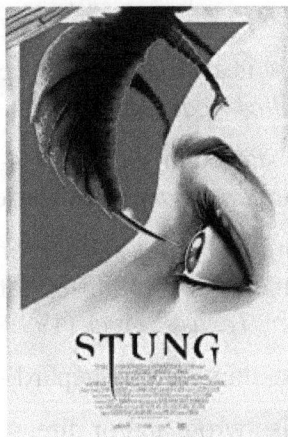

*Story:*

A garden party full of the wealthy business owners turns deadly—when giant mutated wasps begin to snack on them.

*Cool Stuff:*

Lance Henrikson, star of such classics as *Aliens* (1986), *Near Dark* (1987) & *Pumpkinhead* (1988) only spent one week on set.

The film's writers, Adam Aresty, was once a caterer at a party that had a wasp infestation—which prompted the screenplay.

## 2 LAVA 2 LANTULA!

*"Fire Burns… Lava Bites Again!"*

Director – Nick Simon

Writer(s) – Neil Elman / Ashley O'Neil

Starring – Steve Guttenberg / Michael Winslow / Michele Weaver / Marion Ramsey

Distributor – Cinetel Films / Syfy

Release Date – Aug. 6, 2016

*Story:*

Those lava-spewing tarantulas return—and so does Guttenberg and his cohorts.

*Cool Stuff:*

The *Police Academy* gang of actors returns for another round.

Nick Simon also directed *The Girl in the Photographs* (2015).

Neil Elman has written numerous movies—*Caved In* (2006), *I Spit on Your Grave 2* (2013), *Stormageddon* (2015), and *House of the Witch* (2017).

Tahnee Welch—daughter of Raquel Welch—appears as herself.

*Special Mentions:*

## INCREDIBLE SHRINKING MAN (1957)

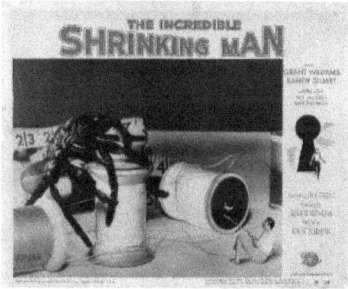

Based on the brilliant novel by Richard Matheson, this film—directed by Jack Arnold—has a brilliant killer spider scene.

The main character, Scott Carey (portrayed by Grant Williams) battles a spider—which, due to Carey's shrinking—is gigantic.

## MYSTERIOUS ISLAND (1961)

Based on the novel by Jules Verne, this film features the brilliant stop-motion effects of Ray Harryhausen.

There are several giant creatures in the film—but it is the giant bees that are relevant to this book.

Two survivors are trapped in a bee nest and we are treated to an incredible scene as one of the bees slowly seals the couple inside.

## CREEPSHOW (1982)

Created by two icons of the genre—written by Stephen King and directed by George A. Romero, this collection of tales is like comic book come to life. It's even presented as one in the framing sequences. Each tale is graphic and creepy, but the one segment relevant to this book features one of the most popular

The final segment, titled *They're Creeping Up On You*. It is the story of a greedy businessman (portrayed by E.G. Marshall), whose secure penthouse is overrun with cockroaches.

## THE LORD OF RINGS: THE RETURN OF THE KING (2003)

The finale of the brilliant trilogy directed by Peter Jackson (based on the books by J.R.R. Tolkien) has a terrifying scene with Frodo and Samwise battling with the giant spider, Shelob.

## THE MIST (2007)

Based on a story by Stephen King, and directed by Frank Darabont, this brilliant—and tragic Horror film—features several creatures that appear during a freak storm. One of the creatures is a giant, wasp-like monster.

## *FINALE*

And so, we come to the end of Creeping Crawling Cinema. It can be a fun little film niche and, when done well, can also provide all the skin-crawling moments that scare us, entertain us, and make for a fun evening with friends and family.

Hey, what's that on the ceiling above you?

## About the Author

Edward Brock has published articles and stories in such publications as—*Antiques & Collecting Magazine, Filmfax, Scary Monsters, G-Fan, Scarlet Street, Halloween Forevermore, Shotgun Horror Clips, AlienSkin* and *Blood Moon Rising*. He also has books (print & eBook) on Amazon, and other platforms.

Find him on

Facebook, Goodreads, Instagram, & Twitter